THE G█████ ONEOTA V█████GE

MARSHALL McKUSICK

COMMENTARY
DAVID A. BAERREIS
ALFRED W. BOWERS
DAVID S. BROSE
HESTER A. DAVIS
HENRY P. FIELD
ELIZABETH J. GLENN
DALE R. HENNING
WILLIAM M. HURLEY
FLOYD G. LOUNSBURY
G. RICHARD PESKE

FAUNAL IDENTIFICATION
HOLMES A. SEMKEN

REPORT 4

OFFICE OF STATE ARCHAEOLOGIST

THE UNIVERSITY OF IOWA, IOWA CITY

1973

THE GRANT ONEOTA VILLAGE by Marshall McKusick
is the fourth of a series of reports.

Established in 1959, the Office of State Archaeologist
has the primary responsibility for the discovery, excavation,
and preservation of antiquities (Iowa Laws 305A). The
State Archaeologist is appointed by the Board of Regents
and serves on the faculty in Anthropology. Headquarters
are at The University of Iowa Archaeological Laboratory,
Iowa City. Beginning in 1970 a series of reports and books
has been issued on various investigations, describing and
interpreting the discoveries. These studies are published
in both hardbound and paperback editions, and should be
ordered from The University of Iowa Department of Publications, Iowa City, Iowa 52242. The prices listed include
postage.

1. *The Davenport Conspiracy* by Marshall McKusick, 1970,
   cloth $5, paperback $3.

2. *The Kingston Oneota Site* by Dean Straffin, 1971,
   cloth $5, paperback $2.

3. *Prehistoric Investigations* by Adrian Anderson and others,
   1971, cloth $5, paperback $3.

4. *The Grant Oneota Village* by Marshall McKusick, 1973,
   cloth $5, paperback $3.

CONTENTS

TABLES

ILLUSTRATIONS

1. CULTURAL SUCCESSION ON THE HARTLEY TERRACE

In the summer of 1970 the accidental discovery of the Grant village uncovered post molds of huge, many-family houses measuring twenty-five feet wide
and up to ninety feet long. It is the first firm evidence of such huge buildings
within the Oneota archaeological tradition; a tradition frequently identified with
the far-ranging Siouan tribes. After reviewing the historical and ethnographic
evidence I am reasonably convinced that the Indians lived in similar longhouses
at summer encampments throughout much of the Upper Mississippi Valley. If
the hypothesis is correct, this first discovery foreshadows substantiating evidence
at future excavations over a wide geographic area. The second contribution of
this report is the definition of the very early Grant type pottery within the Oneota
Tradition, having decorative techniques which are distinctive in both kind and
frequency from those appearing on pottery at the adjacent Lane Enclosure, one
of the definitive sites of the later Allamakee Trailed type. The pottery separation
is supported by the available radiocarbon dates. The dates provide one answer to
a vexing problem raised some years earlier: was the Orr Oneota derived from a
more Middle Mississippian culture in the area? (McKusick 1964: 164). The
evidence so far obtained strongly suggests there was no "pre-Oneota" Mississippian culture within the valley of the Upper Iowa River in northeastern Iowa.
The Hartley Phase people of the Late Woodland Tradition abandoned the fortified encampment on the terrace sometime after A.D. 900, and they were almost
immediately replaced by the Grant Oneota culture. The predecessor of the Orr
Oneota was still earlier Oneota; and it must have originated elsewhere. This
finding supports the interpretation of Carcajou Point in southeastern Wisconsin
made almost a decade ago (Hall 1962). Both he and later authors (Baerreis and
Bryson 1965) interpreted the radiocarbon dates from that site as demonstrating
that by A.D. 1000 Oneota culture had already separated from its Middle Mississippian forebearers. Depending upon the interpretation of radiocarbon dates
from the Dixon site in western Iowa, the Correctionville-Blue Earth Oneota
ceramic series may have separated early, comparable to southeastern Wisconsin.
The Grant village in northeastern Iowa falls within this pattern of early Oneota
separation. The chronology supports the *Baerreis-Bryson hypothesis* that Oneota
expansion occurred during the climatically favorable Neo-Atlantic episode dating
from approximately A.D. 800-1250. This hypothesis challenged earlier views
in American archaeology that Oneota was a very late prehistoric-protohistoric

---

Using the format of *CURRENT ANTHROPOLOGY*, the report was sent to a
number of North American archaeologists. Their evaluations and comments together with
my reply are published together as an addendum to this report. A brief preliminary study has
previously appeared in volume 3, *PREHISTORIC INVESTIGATIONS*, summarizing the pottery description and longhouse discovery (McKusick 1971). Publication costs were defrayed
by a gift from Harriet Lubetkin, former member of the State Board of Regents.

manifestation possibly developing during a period of climatic deterioration which could not support fully developed Middle Mississippian culture (see Gibbon 1970).

There is a proposed classification that the Oneota Tradition can be divided into Emergent, Developmental and Classic horizons, although a temporary alliance of scholars accepting this scheme apparently failed to agree (Hall 1962: 106, Mildred Wedel 1963: 120). The *Hall Oneota Developmental Classification* will continue to prove very difficult to apply. It appears to have theoretical parallels with interpretively named periods for areas of high civilization in Meso-America where historical reconstruction may support such divisions. Those classifications, however, show little uniformity, and the purpose served seems to be explanation to non-regional specialists rather than providing working definitions for critical analysis of relationships. There must be a series of "Emergent Oneota" sites, but the transition may have been rapid and limited in territorial extent. Once the cultural adaptation to the Oneota Tradition was made, in A.D. 800 or 900, it must have proven to be highly successful leading to its subsequent spread across a number of ecological niches in the prairie and woodlands where it had not previously occurred. In any case, the Grant ceramics and structures are best characterized as *emerged* rather than *emergent*. Except for the early dates one could not readily determine whether the village culture was *Developmental* or *Classic*; reinforcing questions foreseen by Mildred Wedel (1963).

In 1960 Griffin hypothesized that the early Oneota Aspect as a group would have rectangular Middle Mississippian wattle and daub houses. *The Griffin hypothesis* is not supported by the Grant village in a major area of Oneota occurrence. To the extent the hypothesis is applicable, the region is elsewhere nearer the Middle Mississippian centers to the south, and presumably earlier in the Neo-Atlantic episode. Even at Carcajou Point, the unique early Oneota rectangular house had no associated daub (Hall 1962: 96), and no other Oneota sites have wattle and daub wall construction. Archaeologists have recognized or inferred the presence of pole frameworks at Oneota sites in various areas of the midwest, and have assumed these were covered with bark or mats. The Grant village excavations indicate this type of construction has a considerable antiquity within the Oneota Tradition. Whether or not the Grant style of summer longhouse will be widely found remains to be seen. The various conclusions expressed in this report must remain provisional, but they may have considerable value as one step towards the current reassessment of Oneota origins, settlements, and subsequent development. This is no small matter, for the prehistoric Oneota Tradition is geographically spread through parts of at least eight states, and in some of them may have spanned seven, eight, or more centuries.

PRELIMINARY ONEOTA SITE DISTRIBUTIONS IN EASTERN IOWA Wherever the Oneota tradition began, it must have been east or south of Iowa, for nowhere in the state does one encounter more abundant Oneota remains than along the Upper Iowa Valley, with a seemingly good chance of time depth and cultural diversity. Yet Oneota is intrusive here, appearing early and without antecedents. The other area of potential Oneota development is southeastern Iowa where surveys are just beginning to obtain information on a number of sites with a still undetermined amount of ceramic differences. Both of these major areas of occurrence show discontinuities with sites reported from central and western Iowa. The Upper Iowa Valley settlements did not extend far upstream, and did not spread into parallel drainage systems to the south. The southeastern settlements are on the Mississippi bluffs or floodplain, and do not show a continuous distribution upstream along the major tributaries. A number of Oneota settlements occurred along the Des Moines in central Iowa; others are in the lake country of northern Iowa and sporadically appear along the Big and Little Sioux Rivers in a few northwestern counties. Oneota pottery occurs in southwestern Iowa, Glenwood Locality, earth lodges; but no major Oneota settlements have been reported. Over the years a number of suggestions have appeared in print about the midwestern relationships of these Oneota manifestations, but the unexpected time depth shown by some radiocarbon dates strongly suggests the need for caution in generalizing about tribal and linguistic identifications, and taxonomic relationships.

In eastern Iowa there is a conspicuous gap in Oneota sites as one travels southward, downstream along the Mississippi past the inlets, bluffs, and tributary streams on the Iowa side. Some Oneota sherds appear in the upper levels of a few rockshelters by the Yellow River, a small stream within the southern limits of Allamakee County in Effigy Mounds National Monument (Orr 1948MS and Logan 1959MS). There are no villages or cemeteries reported from this valley and the Oneota may have visited it only during infrequent hunting trips. The Mouse Hollow Rockshelter on the Maquoketa River had some Middle Mississippian sherds resembling Ramey Incised, but no recognized Oneota sherds (Logan 1959MS). There is no information on Oneota villages in the eastern tier of river counties beginning in the north with Clayton, and continuing through Jackson, Dubuque, Scott, and northern Muscatine. Either sites do not exist or they have not been reported. Oneota sites reappear along the bluffs and terraces between the river towns of Muscatine and Burlington, in the counties of Muscatine, Louisa and Des Moines, a fact first noted by Keyes (*e.g.* 1951: 336). Some southeastern sites are within the Chariton-Kingston ceramic series (Guthrey-Dowell-Kingston) discussed by Henning (1970) and Straffin (1971). These are also related to the Moingoina Phase, named but not yet defined by Gradwohl, which includes a series of components on the Des Moines River near the state capitol. The McKinney site, an octagonal enclosed village near the Toolesboro Hopewell Mounds, is considered a component of the Orr Phase by Henning, but this has been questioned by Straffin and my own examination of the sherds makes me reluctant to identify it with any currently defined phase.

The interior drainage systems appear to show similar discontinuities in Oneota distributions although surveys are very incomplete. It has long been recognized that along the Upper Iowa River virtually all of the major Oneota settlements and cemeteries are in the lower valley fairly near the Mississippi, and they do not occur in the counties of Winneshiek or Howard, inland from Allamakee.* Other inland streams of east central Iowa show the same pattern. I know of no Oneota villages along the Maquoketa, Turkey or Wapsipinicon Valleys, or Catfish Creek by Dubuque. A summary of 100 sites along the Iowa River by Anderson (1971) showed that except for the village near the mouth in southeastern Iowa, very few shell tempered sherds were reported. Two open sites and a rock shelter had some Oneota pottery north of Iowa City, and there were two unconfirmed reports of Oneota pottery at the headwaters in Hancock County, but no major interior settlements are known along this river. The Cedar River, a major watercourse but tributary to the Iowa in its lower reaches, has no reported Oneota village sites. The group of shelters on the Cedar at Palisades Kepler State Park near Cedar Rapids (Logan 1959MS) had a single shell tempered specimen in a series of collections containing some 2,500 Woodland sherds. The preliminary survey by Straffin of the Skunk River, tributary to the Des Moines, has not yet found shell tempered pottery, and the Des Moines River itself has few or no prehistoric Oneota villages until one reaches the central valley near the state capitol.

The precarious results of these preliminary surveys all point in the same direction. Neither the Oneota nor the earlier Woodland cultures show a uniform geographical distribution. Regional diversity is beginning to appear, reflecting the settlement by different, sometimes contemporaneous cultures, each one occupying its own territory along the tributary systems and valley of the Mississippi River. For this reason, generalizations drawn from the Upper Iowa River Valley vary in their application to the surrounding regions.

TERMINOLOGY The word Oneota does not seem to be Winnebago in origin, its probable Iroquoian linguistic derivation resulting from a nineteenth century error by the geologist W. J. McGee. He apparently asked visiting Oneida Iroquois for the Indian name of the Upper Iowa River, and their response, Oneota, has been translated to mean "people who sprang from a rock" (see Mildred Wedel 1959: 6-7). The geological application of the term to a geological formation dates from McGee, the archaeological usage coming later at the suggestion of Charles R. Keyes, and being indirectly taken from a preliminary report by Ellison Orr (1914) who discussed shell tempered pottery from the Oneota or Upper Iowa River. With the development of the Midwestern Taxonomic Method in the 1930s by McKern and others, the Oneota culture of the Upper Iowa Valley was recognized as being related in varying degrees to similar manifestations over a wide area in the midwest. Within the terminology being devel-

*Some Oneota sherds occur in five Winneshiek County sites, but appear to represent seasonal activity from the downstream villages (Clark Mallam, personal communication 1971).

oped, Keyes suggested that the Upper Iowa culture should be named after Ellison Orr. The Orr Focus was classified within the Oneota Aspect, Upper Phase,
of the Mississippian Pattern. Beyond the Upper Iowa other components or close
resemblances were initially recognized by various authors in northern Iowa, eastern Nebraska, southeastern South Dakota and Minnesota, and southwestern Wisconsin (Mildred Mott 1938: 289-304, Hill and Wedel 1936: 41, Keyes 1927: 222-
224, 1951: 325-338, and McKern 1945: 161-163). The pottery from the Upper
Iowa used to establish these relationships was summarized rather than fully described, and while the principal investigators in the midwest were familiar with
it, the more precise quantitative details were lacking.

The publication of *Oneota Sites on the Upper Iowa River* by Mildred Mott
Wedel in 1959 provided the first detailed archaeological descriptions of the excavations, pottery, and artifacts. *Every Oneota component* excavated by Keyes
and Orr in the Upper Iowa Valley—village sites, cemeteries, and Oneota mound
burials—was interpreted as a manifestation of the same culture, the Orr Focus,
and she limited comparisons to sites in the three state corner region of northeastern Iowa, southeastern Minnesota and southwestern Wisconsin. The Midway
site in Wisconsin, originally classified as Orr Focus by McKern, was now seen as
separate, and a problem in classification. The original comparisons of Upper
Iowa with other midwestern components had emphasized both ceramic and cultural *similarities,* but subsequent studies showed that ceramic *differences* were
present, suggesting a number of foci within the Oneota Aspect, and some cultural
traits proved to be non-specific to the Orr Focus, since they had a broader inter-
focus distribution.

Although Mildred Wedel's study bears a 1959 publication date, it is my
recollection that it was not circulated until almost a year later. Meanwhile, Dale
Henning, then a graduate student at The University of Iowa, undertook an
investigation of Oneota pottery from the Correctionville, Dixon, Flatiron and
Lane Enclosure sites; a 1960 M.A. thesis directed by Reynold Ruppe. It was
subsequently published (Henning 1961), providing detailed comparisons on the
Correctionville Trailed and *Allamakee Trailed* pottery types, the second type
name being taken from Mildred Wedel's study. The publication of the Ph.D.
thesis written at the University of Wisconsin by Robert Hall (1962) under the
direction of David Baerreis provided new insights into the development and
antiquity of Oneota culture with implications throughout the midwest. Subsequent research and theories stemmed from Wisconsin, Iowa Oneota being
relatively ignored through the 1960s. Excavations continued but the reports
were not available for comparative studies; David Gradwohl's work in the central
Iowa reservoirs, Amy Harvey at Blood Run, Dale Henning at Correctionville,
and Dean Straffin at Kingston. In 1969 Henning completed his Ph.D. thesis
under David Baerreis on the subject of Oneota sites in central Missouri, somewhat revised for publication the next year. This study formed the typological
and conceptual model for Straffin's thesis and publication in 1971. The report
by Henning (1970) was of immediate relevance to Iowa interpretations because

of radiocarbon dates, and ceramic similarities with villages in the Des Moines Valley and along the southeastern Iowa bluffs by the Mississippi. Moreover, he concluded with the most comprehensive recent study of Oneota pottery and relationships through the midwest. Despite the many solid contributions, Henning's conclusions raise questions over terminological usage in describing relationships of various orders of magnitude.

Within the past decade archaeologists have largely abandoned the Midwestern Taxonomic Method, substituting new terms with a different order of relationships. Hall (1962) named or renamed the Oneota Aspect as the Oneota Tradition,* extending its application through time and cultural transition from Middle Mississippian origins. He retained the focus designation, but these were now viewed as separable entities through time. To interpret the diagram of foci relationships (1962 vol. 2: 121), one might interpret each of Hall's foci as individual sub-traditions emerging from a succession of common branches going back to a common stem and the total development passing through the stage-like horizons of Emergent, Developmental, and Classic. The Orr Focus, for example is plotted back in time to A.D. 1200 to 1300, where it shows a common origin with the Blue Earth Focus, both being part of the Chiwere Sioux linguistic group. This is a far different conception than the discrete, non-temporal ordering of site components originally defined as foci in the Midwestern classification. Henning's later study followed more recent shifts in classification and renamed some of the Hall foci as phases. The Chariton River Oneota sites were now conceived as representing a group continuity, excluding part of the Utz site collections, but no phase designation was named. The Orr Phase was seen as occurring intermittently from eastern Illinois to the plains of eastern Nebraska and Kansas, while within the Upper Iowa Valley it was conceived as being of recent prehistoric origin. Admitted ceramic variability occurred among these widely separated components.

The terminology in growing use lacks the intermediate steps that archaeologists previously developed; a positive step if it avoids the same pitfalls. Unfortunately, in one sense we have gone full circle. Oneota pottery of the Upper Iowa Orr Focus was originally inadequately described and for this reason was widely identified through the midwest. In the middle period of research fuller description showed that the Orr Focus pottery had more restricted occurrences. Now, renamed a phase, Orr is used as a more comprehensive term to cover a wider latitude of ceramic components in the absence of detailed, defined pottery typology for most areas.

The Midwestern Taxonomic Method stressed varying degrees of similarities among related components, deliberately excluding the problems of chronological componential sequence. In part this reflected the absence of radiocarbon dating. However, newer replacement terminology as applied to Oneota studies has yet

---

*All named taxonomic units are capitalized in our report. Usage varies and many prefer not to capitalize these terms. Our lower case usage includes the terms site, village, type, and component; usage most extend to the non-MTM phase taxon.

to demonstrate that the chronological succession and intergroup relationships can be clearly defined. The groupings themselves are becoming too broad. Similarities between Grant and later pottery might be judged to have a relationship—let us say a *group continuity* lacking presently known intervening steps. Such a judgment would extend the Orr Phase to seven centuries with other recognized, but dangling components, from Illinois to Nebraska. This latter terminology has its uses, but is not helpful in the present study.

This report uses the following terminology. The *Oneota Tradition* includes all Upper Mississippian cultures defined as Oneota by archaeologists since 1959, these cultural manifestations being separable from Middle Mississippian phases. The *Orr Phase* follows Henning's 1970 usage to include the specific variety of components he has stated are related. While this classification has value for broad interpretations, its time depth may present a linguistic trap, and the various Siouan linguistic groups—Chiwere, Dhegiha, Santee and others—are kept separate from the Orr Phase which is defined by ceramics. In some contexts I have used the term Orr *ceramic series* as a preferable substitute for Henning's Orr Phase. If we look at the Grant village pottery as a member of a broader group it has characteristics which might put it within the Orr ceramic series, but such a classification has limited descriptive advantages when defining its distinctive traits. For this reason the Upper Iowa Oneota pottery (once the center of the Orr Focus) is now referred to as *Allamakee Trailed type,* and the *Grant type* is distinguished from it. For descriptive purposes our Lane Enclosure pottery sample is compared with Grant pottery to illustrate contrasting traits. Other pottery from the Lane Enclosure was one of the major groups forming the basis for the original Allamakee Trailed definitions. The review of the various substantial Oneota collections from the Upper Iowa has been deferred to a later study.

HARTLEY TERRACE SITES   The Grant site lies on the Hartley Terrace, a major settlement area for Oneota and earlier Woodland cultures. The terrace is an isolated remnant, largely composed of sand, lying approximately north-south with prominent peaks at either end (figure 1).* The western side is bounded by French Creek joining the Upper Iowa which circles the terrace to the north. The eastern length of the terrace is more or less isolated by an ancient channel of the Upper Iowa, part of the depression forming two small ponds. The terrace is easily accessible from below around much of its perimeter, but nevertheless provided several defensible locations, and from it one can look upstream along the valley of the Upper Iowa for many miles or downstream to the Wisconsin bluffs of the Mississippi River.

The major site areas all occur on the north half of the terrace, the southern half, with no reported surface evidence of occupation, requires more systematic testing. The first archaeological map on the terrace was prepared by Colonel P.

---

*Tables and figures follow the list of references at the back of this report.

W. Norris, in 1882, working under the general direction of Cyrus Thomas of the Bureau of American Ethnology, Smithsonian Institution. Colonel Norris energetically contacted local collectors along both sides of the Mississippi River, and dug at a number of the more interesting sites. His surveys and discussions provided information difficult to evaluate today, but it may be noted in passing that his shrewd interest in the startling finds of hieroglyphic tablets and elephant effigy pipes reported by Reverend Gass of the Davenport Academy led to Tiffany's correspondence broaching the scandal of relic fabrication. He thus deserves credit for helping to resolve a major series of hoaxes. Colonel Norris died unexpectedly after the Iowa investigations and his excavation reports were later published by Thomas (1887, 1894). The two maps of the terrace sites are of interest, despite inaccuracies, because they contain information available from no other source. The general plan of the terrace by Norris shows a number of sites (figure 2). Using their modern names, they are: (A) the Lane Enclosure, (B) the Lane Mounds, (C) three unnamed burial mounds on top of Brown's Hill, (D) the Hartley Fort, (E) an unnamed enclosure which neither Ellison Orr nor I was able to relocate, and (F) a stone burial chamber. The "Little Iowa River" is the Upper Iowa River. The terrace outlines are greatly in error, and a better orientation is obtained by rotating his north arrow nearly 40 degrees east.

A more representative view of the terrace sites appears as figure 3, redrawn from one of Ellison Orr's maps with additional information added. The four major sites are the Hartley Fort, Lane Mounds, Grant village, and Lane Enclosure. Three sites noted by Norris do not appear on this map. The three mounds on top of Brown's Hill have been destroyed. The unlocated enclosure, now destroyed, probably lay in an area by the ridge south of the Lane Mounds overlooking the ponds. On figure 3, this would be the area of short east-west fence, extending north to the map designation 13AM-104. The stone burial chamber location is uncertain, but adjusting the Norris map orientation radically, it seemingly lay on the north slope of the terrace, between and north of mounds 13 and 5. In 1970 we found a few fragments of human cranium eroding from the bank north of Mound 5, and other burials are probably present along that edge of the terrace.

The Lane Mounds named for a former landowner reportedly contained eighty-two round and five linear mounds when they were mapped and tested by Colonel Norris in 1882 (Thomas 1887, 1894). Ten surviving mounds, greatly reduced by cultivation, were excavated in 1934 and 1936 (Index in Orr 1963). He found both Woodland and Oneota burials with representative associated pottery and other artifacts. The Woodland pottery is described by Logan (1959MS) and Mildred Wedel (1959) summarizes the Oneota grave finds from these mounds.

The Hartley Fort is a small earthwork outlining a square area, about 150 feet to a side, with associated mounds and borrow pits. Excavations in 1964 demonstrated that the site was a small Late Woodland settlement surrounded by a stockade of posts set into the subsoil. The posts, identified from post molds, averaged six to eight inches in diameter, placed at intervals on centers of about eighteen inches, with an overlapping stockaded entryway located on the east side. The surrounding earthwork was identified as the rampart; soil heaped against the stockade to strengthen the setting of the posts and perhaps originally designed to provide cover for archers defending the camp. The Late Woodland fortified settlement is the type site of the Hartley Phase, and possibly dates from about A.D. 900. Strong Mississippian influences are evident; side notched triangular projectile points, and trade pottery of Middle Mississippian origin. The Late Woodland pottery is of two types. One is a variety of Lake Michigan Ware. The Hartley Plain type is vaguely reminiscent of the Mill Creek Chamberlain and Great Oasis varieties found in northwest Iowa and elsewhere. The abandonment of the fortified camp by the Hartley culture may have been caused by pressures from new arrivals, cultural bearers of the Oneota Tradition. The mounds associated with the ramparts were later additions and not of Woodland origin. They contained Oneota burials in several instances overlying the former stockade. A preliminary report has appeared (McKusick 1964a) and a more detailed analysis will be published in this monograph series. The Hartley Fort is of major importance in interpreting the cultural replacement of Late Woodland by the Oneota Tradition and fortunately the landowner, Grant Hartley, dedicated the site as part of the State Preserve System in 1970 to provide protection and control future excavation.

The Lane Mounds and Hartley Fort are predominantly Woodland Tradition sites with later Oneota intrusions. The other two major sites on the terrace are Oneota villages. The *Grant village* named for Grant Hartley, lies on the northern periphery of the Lane Mounds group, between Mounds 14 and 2 with other mounds unreported by Orr present. In relation to the Norris map (figure 2), Mound 14 may be the linear indicated in the second row-east, seventh mound from the top. Occupied after A.D. 1000, the village was a small compact Oneota settlement, a summer camp about one acre in size. The Indians lived in multifamily longhouses, built of poles, and covered by mats or bark. The camp was not fortified.

The fourth site of importance on the terrace is the *Lane Enclosure,* variously named the Lane site, Pottery Circle, and Old Fort. It is a controversial, circular embankment enclosing a small, compact, Oneota village one acre in size. Excavation in the north rampart during the summer of 1970 failed to completely resolve the question of fortifications first raised almost a century ago. A suggestion of palisade post molds occurred in subsoil underlying the midline of the rampart, but the evidence is not conclusive and further work is needed to clarify the nature of the defensive works at other points of the site perimeter. The Lane Enclosure, occupied from late prehistoric into early protohistoric times, contained several items of European origin.

The four sites of the Hartley Terrace have a probable time span of fifteen centuries, and illustrate the major cultural changes occurring in the region from Woodland culture through the period of first aboriginal contact with the French explorers. The Hartley Terrace provides a unique record of prehistoric structures and events not easily duplicated in the Upper Mississippi Valley.

RADIOCARBON DATES   Twelve dates suggest the relative chronological positions of the major site occupations (figure 4). The determinations were made by Geochron Laboratories, Cambridge, Massachusetts, in the late fall of 1970.

The Hartley Fort clearly had two components and this was initially stressed in my preliminary report (1964a). The Late Woodland occupation built the earthwork and stockade. The published estimate without benefit of C14 suggested the settlement was about A.D. 1200. A date of A.D. 960 ± 100 (GX-2002) is from excavation unit S-3, south stockade. A storage pit inside the stockade, feature 2-1, contained indigenous Late Woodland sherds with some rolled rim, Middle Mississippi trade sherds, together with several corn kernels. This sample dates A.D. 870 ± 95 (GX-1997). These two dates suggest an occupation near the beginning of the tenth century, three hundred years earlier than the estimate.

From extensive excavations in the south rampart it was clear that long after the abandonment of the fort, it was reused for burials by later Oneota Indians. This is described in the original report, the most conclusive evidence being rock cairns placed over burials which covered the earlier post molds. Mortuary pottery associated with these burials was either miniature pots or larger oval bowls, typical of the Allamakee Trailed type. A date from charcoal associated with Oneota burial 5, unit S-1, south stockade, is A.D. 1480 ± 120 (GX-2000). This date shown on figure 4 in a separate column, fits with the early Lane Enclosure dates and these burials do not seem to be identified with the Grant village. The second date 1290 ± 120 (GX-1998) is from a storage pit N2, north rampart, which occurred just inside the stockade line. The date is tentatively placed within the Oneota reoccupation, although this raises some difficulties and additional determinations are required.

The Grant Village contained burials attributed to the Woodland mounds, but the radiocarbon samples come from Oneota storage pits. A date of A.D. 980 ± 95 (GX-1996) comes from cache pit 27 which lay adjacent and outside the west wall of House 8, in the east house area. A second date A.D. 1005 ± 115 (GX-1995) is from cache pit 19 in the west house area, by the lines of posts attributed to Houses 1 and 2. The date A.D. 1080 ± 180 (GX-1994) is from cache pit 12 in the wall line of House 6, although it might more appropriately be assigned to the floor area encompassed by either House 3 or 5. The three Grant dates are close together and indicate the Oneota village flourished sometime during the eleventh century.

The Lane Enclosure dates suggest two periods of occupation, one in the fifteenth century and resettlement in the seventeenth century. All five samples date the Allamakee Trailed grouping of Oneota ceramics. Samples A.D. 1460 ± 85 and 1475 ± 95 (GX-1993 and 1989) coincide with the intrusive Oneota burials at the Hartley Fort. The later dates 1620 ± 90, 1690 ± 90, and 1740 ± 160 (GX-1992, 1990 and 1991), are not inconsistent with an early period of contact.

It is well known that during the voyage of discovery by Joliet and Marquette, they reported trade guns in the Indian village visited in Iowa during 1673; the trade extending in advance of the explorations themselves. The 1690 carbon date is from a cache pit which contained several small pieces of brass and iron. The 1740 date is later than one would expect given the paucity of trade items at the site, but the determination was made from a small charcoal sample giving a wider date range.

For the purposes of this report the chronological placement of the Grant site follows closely upon the abandonment of the fortified Late Woodland encampment and precedes the construction of the Lane Enclosure. The Grant dates seem to fit both theories and growing evidence from other areas of Oneota development.

2. ARCHAEOLOGY: DISCOVERY OF PREHISTORIC LONGHOUSES

The northern edge of the Lane Mound group shows two perceptible rises of an artificial character initially assumed to be the embankment remnants of the Lane Enclosure. Excavations encountered Oneota storage pits underlying a plow zone almost lacking in cultural remains. The decorated rims did not fit into the typical Oneota series for the area, and shortly afterwards the correct location of the Lane Enclosure was confirmed by test trenches an eighth of a mile away which located Orr's 1936 excavations.* The fortuitous discovery of the Grant site suggests that other early sites may lie somewhat more buried, or be inconspicuous compared with the later Oneota villages in the Upper Iowa Valley. The Grant excavation plan (figure 5) shows the two main parallel trenches, A and B, running west to east to cut through the mounds on both sides of the village area. Each trench was laid out in ten foot squares, which in my experience are much more suitable than the five foot squares for uncovering structures. The west fifty feet of Trench A encountered a refilled ditch in the middle of the linear mound, and human secondary burial groups A to D. In the second fifty feet very little occupational debris occurred and the trench was discontinued after reaching culturally sterile subsoil.

Trench B encountered the same refilled ditch in the linear mound and near the eastern edge, post molds of substantial houses. The trench continued a total distance of 320 feet crossing the central area of the site which lacked structures, crossing an eastern habitation area with a house line and storage pits, and was discontinued after it passed beyond the village periphery. A bulldozer provided by the Allamakee County Board of Supervisors for clearing and backfill during the excavation, was used for exploratory trenches determining the extent of the ditch in the linear mound, and the area of Oneota habitation. These trenches, marked T on the plan, together with extensive clearing of structure outlines, provide a unique body of data on the organization of an Oneota village. Ex-

---

*My crew of nine University of Iowa graduate and undergraduate students worked six weeks at the Lane Enclosure and Grant sites, but the scale of excavations required additional help. The project could not have been carried out in its final form without Jerry Clark, former Instructor of Anthropology and Sociology at Luther College, who discontinued his Oneota excavations at the Blake Farm site and generously placed both himself and his crew of Luther students at my disposal. Luther College also provided laboratory space and housing facilities. The basic research was funded by the state archaeological appropriation, but the significance of the finds was so apparent that a more intensive study was required. The extension of field work was made possible by emergency funding provided by the State Executive Council, supported by Governor Robert Ray. With the combined crews and assistants, we had over thirty engaged on the project during the crucial period of extending the trenching.

cavation techniques varied. A representative section away from mound areas contained three principal layers; pure sand at the base, merging upward into a sandy, compact, yellow loess, and overlaid by an upper layer of sandy dark humus. The humus layer, averaging a foot thick included the plow zone. Village debris was so sparse that this layer was shoveled off to unmixed loess, which was repeatedly skim-shoveled and troweled to expose outlines of post holes, numerous rodent burrows, and storage pits. Rare sherds, chipping waste, and irregular chunks of fire burned, dolomitic limestone found in the humus layer seemed to occur for the most part in association with underlying storage pits. As previously mentioned the site was discovered by accident, previous investigators on the terrace having no knowledge of its existence, and this is a reflection of the very sparse cultural material in the upper layer. Several severe rainstorms hindered the excavation of the storage pits. Despite this difficulty virtually all storage pits were cleared by shoveling and troweling, the earth then passed through quarter-inch screen. As a control, fill from storage pit 13 was totally removed in plastic bags and taken to the Archaeological Laboratory at Luther College where the earth was washed through window screen mesh. No technique we tried markedly increased the very sparse artifact yield. Figures 44 to 52 show eighteen photographs of excavated features, burials, and houses, which should be reviewed prior to reading the following description of the work.

REMAINS ATTRIBUTED TO THE WOODLAND TRADITION The Grant site overlay parts of two older mounds and one would anticipate some evidence of Woodland culture to be mixed in the later Oneota settlement. There was surprisingly little Woodland material except for undated burials, none of the series having diagnostic associated artifacts. Mound 14, an oval or linear mound was apparently mapped by both Norris and later by Orr, although the correlation raises some problems. Cultivation has reduced its original height to less than a foot and its exact peripheries are now impossible to define. The trench cuts showed a refilled ditch with sloping sides lying on a north-south axis through the length of the mound (figure 44). Profiles were mapped on both side walls of each trench, although none of these are illustrated because of the identification of the ditch as fairly recent disturbance. The ditch fill was almost totally sterile in cultural materials. No Woodland sherds occurred, and only a few Oneota sherds and some shell and animal bones were found. Two small undecorated Oneota body sherds were present at the base of the ditch fill in trench B. These minor finds are attributed to backfilling the original ditch.

This ditch, clearly visible in the A and B trenches, sixty-five feet apart, could not have been a stockade trench associated with the Oneota village. Testing beyond the south perimeter of the mound with bulldozer cuts found no further trace of the ditch, it being limited to the mound itself. It does not seem related to Woodland construction of the mound since it had neither burials nor cultural remains of that tradition, and no similar mound features have been reported in the area. The most reasonable explanation is that the refilled ditch is an unrecorded archaeological excavation. Colonel Norris working at this site for the Smithsonian Institution in 1882 "pretty thoroughly overhauled" nearly twenty mounds and a section of the Lane Enclosure—all in two days using a plow and a crew of farmers (Mildred Wedel 1959: 10, citing Norris 1882MS). It would appear that the destruction of the internal length of the mound resulted from his endeavors.

Burials noted on the excavation plan occurred in both mounds and in the subsoil underlying the houses. In the other Lane Mounds Orr reports the presence of both Oneota and Woodland burials, but many burials lacked artifacts and could not be clearly associated with either group. The Grant site human bone had deteriorated to such an extent that it seems reasonable to attribute it to the Woodland period, later Oneota interments generally being in much better condition. Burial information is summarized in table 2. Both secondary and primary burials have been found in Oneota village sites, often without identifying artifacts. Examples of Oneota re-articulated burials from the Upper Iowa also occur (Henning and Peterson 1965). Variability in both Oneota and Woodland burial practices make it impossible to definitely assign this burial series to either culture.

One incomplete, but restorable, Woodland pot occurred in square C7, of a type defined by Logan (1959MS) as Lane Farm Cord Impressed (figure 42). The pot has a conical base and cord roughened exterior with rocker stamping, neck decoration made by parallel single cord impressed lines over a cord roughened surface finish. This pot may have been a mortuary offering although it was not directly associated with any burial. One other rimsherd of the same type appeared in the fill of storage pit 4, presumably an accidental inclusion. Four grit tempered, cord marked, body sherds were found in various B trench squares, and 10 others occurred in 4 Oneota storage pits. Three projectile points are of presumed Woodland origin; one came from a longhouse post hole and two were in fill from storage pit 24. Straffin (1971) found Woodland-type projectile points in the fill of two storage pits at the Oneota Kingston site, and suggests that these forms are an integral but minor trait of its Oneota lithic assemblage. While this is reasonable, the Oneota might have collected points they found at earlier Woodland sites.

LONGHOUSES When the first post rows formed a square corner in trench B, I anticipated finding small rectangular house outlines closely similar to the single Oneota house at Carcajou Point in Wisconsin isolated by Robert Hall (1962: 17-18 and his plate 4). The lines of post molds were followed by extensive trenching and unexpectedly showed houses of immense size, multi-family dwellings sixty to ninety feet long and twenty-five feet wide. The series of houses appears to have resulted from periodic, probably seasonal rebuilding, reusing standing posts from earlier dwellings, and complex patterns finally emerged in the archaeological excavations. They are analogous, but much larger than the oval ended house patterns associated with Oneota sites in the Chicago area. The Anker and Oak Forest houses varied from 25 to 55 feet long, averaging 13 feet wide (Bluhm *et al.,* 1961). These provide construction and shape parallels, but average about one-fourth the floor area of the Grant houses.

Post molds, commonly encountered in archaeological investigations, result from logs being set into subsoil. During the abandonment or destruction of the structure, its supporting posts burned, were pulled out for reuse, or eventually rotted away. In any case the original hole in subsoil filled with darker humus; and when the subsoil is scraped cleanly, the post molds appear on the excavation floor as round, dark circles, contrasting in color and texture from the surrounding lighter colored, more compact subsoil. Old rodent burrows in the subsoil and possible decayed tree roots also filled with humus and sometimes gave the appearance of post molds. In the excavations the rodent burrows were distinguished by irregular outlines, lack of vertical position, differences in color and texture, and lack of regular spacing. The wall posts forming the sides of the longhouses were large and lay in predictable rows, so that when one group was exposed and marked with wooden stakes, the re-examination or extension of excavated areas found other post molds in line. The posts were pointed at the base and were set 24 to 30 inches deep although very few were cross sectioned because of the time required to clear such large areas. The great majority of side wall posts varied from three to eight inches in diameter, the majority being relatively small, four inch holes. Frequently, burned rocks from fire hearths had been edged into the post holes to strengthen the set of the posts. The rodent burrows were frequently filled with very dark soil in contrast to the post molds which were commonly of a lighter greyish color. The post holes often contained flecks of charcoal, and rarely a stray potsherd or small animal bone fragment seemingly raising the suggestion that some of the posts had been pulled out during the occupation of the site and debris had fallen into the vacant hole. No charred post stumps occurred.

The predictability of spacing, size, and shape simplified the problem of identifying the post molds of the house sides, and no problems arose except in cases where rodent burrows partially obliterated them. Much greater difficulty was encountered with the rounded ends of the longhouses, which had shallower posts more easily confused with rodent burrows. It was impossible to delineate all of the house ends in a completely satisfactory manner. The individual post diameters appear on the plans providing comparative information for archaeologists encountering similar structures.

No comparable houses have been previously reported from the region causing initial difficulties in excavation planning because of the immense size of the structures. The main trench B encountered post lines running diagonally to the excavation and a second series of squares, numbered and prefixed C, was laid out adjacent to the main trench on the south, expanding the cleared area by an additional forty by ten feet. When the house outlines did not turn corners or emerge as small neat square or rectangular structures, the main lines of posts were followed by trenching, outlining what was originally believed to be a single structure. The ten foot square grid system was abandoned in the search for the house perimeters because the houses lay southeast and northeast in orientation and the grid system was east-west, creating diagonal wastage in locating the post lines. The major house lines in the B trench were followed south for a total distance of 120 feet in squares and parallel five foot wide trenches. The south end of the house area terminated in a pattern of posts showing a structure with a rounded end. This was unexpected at the time. In B trench two major side walls of houses had crossed at right angles. Until this was clarified by more extensive clearing, it was mistakenly interpreted as a square-ended house (figures 49, 51).

The initial excavation of the structures thus outlined what appeared to be a 120 foot longhouse with one square and one rounded end, the entire center being isolated by trenching, but as yet unexcavated. The house lines north of the B trench were then followed and a structure with two rounded ends, sixty-five feet long, was isolated. This suggested that our south trenching had uncovered a group of houses rather than a single structure. Working with a reduced crew, it was impossible to shift backdirt and clear a thirty foot wide, eighty foot long area, and the bulldozer removed the overlying earth of the central area. The need to preserve our post lines made it necessary to remove the fill over a single trench crossing; repeated backing and cutting by the belt tracks compacted the subsoil, and subsequent rains and sun baking made parts of the interior area very difficult to skim shovel or trowel. Some interior support posts and small end posts may be incompletely located on the plans for this reason.

The plan shows the final interpretation of the house lines (figure 7). As the major outlines of the houses became clearer during the course of the work, previously missing posts were located. Post molds appear most clearly in fresh cuts, fading as the sun bakes the subsoil. Our most effective clearing was carried out in the morning, and a freshly skimmed surface was often covered by a sheet of black plastic which preserved soil moisture until the area could be more carefully troweled the following day. Ant hills which appeared on previously cleared, sun-baked surfaces, were carefully examined each morning since those in post molds had a darker color than when they occurred over unmixed subsoil; a number of previously overlooked or unmarked posts were located in this way. The post molds faded or were obscured by walking over them, making it necessary to circle the outlines immediately and mark them with wooden stakes. The top of each was color coded with spray paint to check for missing post molds, the gaps being somewhat difficult to visualize in the more complex areas of overlapping houses.

IDENTIFICATION OF HOUSE STRUCTURES   The original field plans are on grid paper at a scale of two feet to an inch, and then photographically reduced. The overall view of the west house area post patterns and features appears as figure 6. The key letters A and B appearing at the left show the relationships of enlarged partial views prepared in drawings 8, 9, and 10. The identification of house structures is proposed in figure 7. The primary purpose of the larger scale drawings, 8, 9, and 10, is to show post diameters and details of construction. The diameters are approximate, that is, rounded off to the nearest inch and no attempt is made to show differences which sometimes occurred between east-west and north-south diameters of a single post. The dimensions of the posts became less with increasing depth. There is of necessity an element of evaluation and judgment in the dimensions, but they are nevertheless included as a guide to future excavations.

Post mold patterns indicate repeated rebuildings and reoccupations at the Grant settlement. My interpretation of the house plans is indicated by the connecting lines drawn beside the posts. These lines represent a few compromises and it is recognized that differences of opinion may result from a study of the plans, particularly over the interpretation of incomplete houses. Outlines for a number of houses are so clear that no question should remain over the house type and dimensions (table 3).

Houses 1 and 2 overlap to a considerable extent but it is possible to show that the wall lines separate along the entire west side extending into the rounded ends on the north and south. This separation demonstrates that House 1 is two feet narrower. A section of the west wall of House 1 could not be located. The separation of these two structures is further confirmed by post spacing; single walls having gaps between posts averaging eighteen inches while lines of overlapping wall posts show closer spacing. The west wall of each house bows out slightly. Very large center support posts are conspicuous in the south end of each house and their number again suggests the separation of these houses. An alternative explanation is that Houses 1 and 2 represent a single structure, the west wall of House 1 being interior bench supports. This explanation is supported by the otherwise unexplained gap in the west wall of House 1 and makes it unnecessary to explain why the two houses, built successively, overlap and share such similar dimensions. I prefer the first interpretation, as it accounts for the multiple support posts and closer spacing on the east side of the two structures. The parallels in construction can be explained by assuming that the two houses followed each other so closely in time that posts which remained standing from the earlier house, were reused to some extent in the later house. From the plan there is no clear evidence as to which house was built first, a problem which also remains unanswered when studying the other overlapping houses at the Grant site. House 2A is a line of posts suggesting a rebuilt end wall.

House 3, largest of the structures, is nearly ninety feet long. The short superfluous section, identified as House 3A, appears to represent a partial reconstruction or rebuilding of the wall. Support posts, centrally located, appear in the northern part of this house. House end 3B is an unclear oval line, somewhat flatter than most of the house ends. It is attributed to one stage in the construction of House 3 possibly correlated with the rebuilding 3A. House 3 possibly began as a somewhat smaller structure later enlarged to 88 feet, or the opposite may have occurred.

House 4, an incomplete house section, has a different orientation than any of the other structures. The west wall line was traced with great difficulty and no trace existed of the east wall which should have crossed trench B.

House 5, cleared for much of its perimeter, was not completely excavated because of substantial backdirt piles. The section 5A is a redundant line of posts which seems to represent rebuilding at the end of the house.

House 6, the second largest house defined, was seventy-five feet long, and its breadth of thirty feet is enormous. Central support posts are well defined in the excavated area, being particularly numerous in the overlap with House 5. Wall lines demonstrate that Houses 5 and 6 are distinctly separate structures but superimposed with the same orientation.

House 7 is incomplete being identified from the post line of the rounded end. It merged in the wall line shared with House 3, and seems to turn at the south end in the series of posts shared with House 2. If this alignment is correct, House 7 is only twenty feet wide, narrowest of the houses. Its probable length of seventy-six feet is calculated by measuring the maximum distance of the north end to the south turn at its juncture with House 2 and adding four feet to project its end.

House 8 lies at the east side of the settlement separated from the west house by the open village center. The structure was identified by one section of its wall, the post duplication suggesting either rebuilding or superimposed houses. Extensive storage pits appeared in the trench where the projected west post wall should have occurred (figure 11).

Hundreds of feet of post lines were traced and mapped. If one adds to this figure the combined estimated lengths of house walls sharing a single line, more than thirteen hundred lineal feet of outside house walls were followed. An effort was made to locate post molds in the highest possible level where they could be seen in the subsoil. During all of this excavation no trace of a builder's trench appeared along any post line.

No occupational debris suggesting a living surface appeared in any excavation of post lines. The original floor of the houses must have been at the ground surface, subsequently destroyed by plowing the site. No trace of lower floor occupational debris was found equivalent to floor levels in semi-subterranean earth lodges associated with Mill Creek and Glenwood-Nebraska cultures found in western Iowa. In two areas, near the center of the site, dark horizontal stains two inches thick occurred at a depth of one foot in the border between plow zone humus and subsoil. These stains, about twelve feet across, may have been living surfaces but did not contain artifacts or refuse, and the adjacent trench squares found no post holes associated with these possible living surfaces.

THE QUESTION OF FORTIFICATIONS   Reviewing a preliminary version of this manuscript, David Baerreis wrote: "The house maps are very difficult to interpret and one certainly wishes that the entire village could have been stripped to reveal the total plan. Do you think there is a possibility that a number of houses were attached to a continuous outer wall that might have enclosed the settlement?" Because of sequential bracketing of the Grant site, between a fortified Late Woodland encampment and the later and apparently fortified Oneota Lane Enclosure, one might also anticipate defensive works at this village. Two fortifications on the terrace show that the lower valley of the Upper Iowa was at times territorially unstable. The excavation was laid out to locate defensive works at the Grant site, but no indication of them appeared.

In review, the low rise on the west contained apparent Woodland secondary burials and was identified as the remnant of a linear, Mound 14, rather than a fortification embankment. The internal lengthwise ditch, ascribed to Col. Norris may have resulted from another archaeological exploratory excavation but there is no evidence to associate it with either Woodland or Oneota occupation. The ditch did not continue south of the mound into the T trench series, but was an isolated rather than enclosing feature. Also on the west, the A trench with a combined length of 120 feet, 10 feet wide, located a few storage pits but neither houses nor stockade posts.

The east house area is harder to interpret, but the trench passed eastwards well beyond the storage pit area without encountering a stockade. The posts identified as the west wall of House 8 (figure 11) do not seem to be a stockade because of the hearth and storage pits beyond them to the east, which would then lie outside the fortification itself. At the Wittrock Mill Creek site we repeatedly located storage pits just inside the stockade wall, but none of them were outside it. The Lane Enclosure storage pits were heavily clustered along the inner rampart, and those few in the rampart center or beyond may be an earlier occupation before the fortification was established. The Woodland occupation at the Hartley fort was similarly within the enclosure. It is possible that the west house area had a stockade connecting the outer walls, but this may be countered with the argument that Iroquois stockades were always set apart from the fragile and flammable houses. The B trench passes beyond both sides of the houses without finding any line of posts which could not be assigned to a house-like structure. I wish I could present the total village plan, and suggestions are presented in Chapter 5. Using the available evidence, longhouses built by the Siouan speaking Winnebago, Quapaw, Osage, Kansa, Santee, and possibly Ioway, provide examples resembling the Oneota houses at the Grant site. These historical and ethnographic parallels provide a descriptive base for interpreting the archaeological evidence. The overlapping walls make the plans difficult to interpret, but there are examples of Osage and Kansa houses built so closely together that it was difficult to pass between them, and the overlapping post line can be interpreted as reuse of former standing posts. If a stockade was present I have been unable to identify it.

3. HISTORY: EXPLORERS AND LONGHOUSES AMONG SIOUAN TRIBES

The Winnebago and their close linguistic relative the Ioway built, lived in, or remembered a remarkable range of house types. The Ioway built earth lodges, wattle and daub houses, square bark houses, oval mat-covered lodges, and buffalo skin tipis (Skinner 1926: 271-277). Winnebago houses summarized by Paul Radin (1923: 104-106) included: the round lodge, long lodge, tipi, grass lodge, gable lodge, platform lodge, ceremonial lodge, and sweat lodge. The diversity of housing resulted from (A) the prehistoric contact with various cultural traditions, (B) historically documented changes brought about by shifts in life style, (C) the relocation of forest and prairie tribes to a plains environment as a result of frontier pressures, (D) the need for special purpose structures, and (E) the seasonal round of activity which made it useful to have different winter and summer houses, as well as temporary shelters used while engaged in food gathering and hunting away from the main settlements.

The first recognition of the specialized nature of archaeological sites in Iowa appears in a very early publication by Frederick Starr (1897a: 340-343) who published a list of site types derived from his ethnographic and archaeological fieldwork: mounds, earthworks, shell-heaps, village sites, rockshelters, aboriginal workshops, quarries, cliff carvings or paintings, and isolated caches. This list influenced the writings of Charles Keyes who used it in organizing his discussions (e.g. "Ancient Sites" in Keyes 1927: 200-214, and 1951: 301-317). The list by Keyes was further expanded in the discussion of site variety (McKusick 1964: 17-29) although at the time I was unaware of its origin from Starr. These various discussions lacked a clear perspective of the yearly subsistence cycle. More recent work elsewhere has begun to differentiate seasonal settlements; for example in Illinois, Struever (1968) has emphasized changes in patterns of Woodland subsistence-settlement systems, and identified specific occupations such as summer agricultural camps and other site distributions within the context of natural food resource exploitation.

Oneota research in Iowa has not yet attempted to perceive a coherent pattern in site distribution, the main reason being that most of the data and conclusions are derived from the excavations by Ellison Orr in the 1930s as part of the long dormant Iowa Archaeological Survey.* The evidence obtained was very selective in nature, Orr being untrained in evaluating structural evidence and

---

*A review of the work of the former Iowa Archaeological Survey, and Orr's contribution to it can be found in Logan (1959MS), Mildred Mott Wedel (1959, 1961), and McKusick (1963, 1971b). These authors are not in complete agreement on several matters, but all acknowledge the substantial contributions of Charles R. Keyes and Ellison Orr which laid the foundation for later research.

rarely saved human skeletal material from burials, or any animal bone except obviously modified artifacts. The systematic identification and evaluation of faunal and floral remains has been a recent development, requiring specializations unavailable in the 1930s, and not yet systematically applied. When it is, we may anticipate a much more fully developed and detailed integrated picture of cultural adaptation to the environmental diversity and resources. Oneota sites along the Upper Iowa should reflect a cyclical series of settlements, based upon the seasonal subsistence activities, and the following provisional comments may provide some order to subsequent research and surveys. From spring into the fall, the Oneota cultivated the terraces, living in *summer villages* of which the Grant site may be one of several possible variations, as longhouses are particularly suited to residential lineages. The various *rock crevices* contain petroglyphs, but no occupational debris. There is growing evidence from stylistic analysis that these petroglyph sites can be mainly attributed to the prehistoric Oneota (McKusick 1971a). There is no known way to determine the time of year when these crevice drawings were made. *Rock shelters* are wider than the usual petroglyph crevices. In reviewing and interpreting the archaeology Logan (1959MS: 86) wrote: "A great many of the local shelters appear to have been occupied at one time or another by prehistoric peoples. From the standpoint of a study focusing on Woodland archaeology, they are very important for they seem to have been occupied most heavily during these earlier stages of local cultural development. In Allamakee County, for example, the bulk of remains assignable to protohistoric and early historic times is found in large village sites on open river terraces. Only a meager amount of material in the top levels of the shelters is assignable to this period". A review of the shelter excavations shows Oneota sherds in the upper levels, but seldom in quantity and my impression supports Logan that comparatively little use was made of this site type by the Oneota. These shelters probably provided a few travelers with temporary protection during food collecting and hunting trips. Orr reported a number of *enclosures* near the mouth of the Upper Iowa Valley, but most of these can only be relocated with difficulty and have never been archaeologically investigated. They are all probable fortifications, and some may well be Oneota in origin, reflecting a potentially complex problem if there was a seasonal settlement pattern and this pattern changed through time. *Quarries, workshops* and small temporary *open camps* have not been identified which is not surprising since most of the Oneota investigations have been directed at large villages and burial areas. Two main Oneota burial patterns occur along the Upper Iowa. The reuse of older *Woodland burial mounds* has been repeatedly demonstrated, and even the apparent construction of additional *Oneota mounds* can be inferred (Mildred Wedel 1959: 18, 28, 30). The second pattern is burials in small *cemeteries* such as the Flynn site (Bray 1961), O'Regan Cemetery, and the Elephant Cemetery (Mildred Wedel 1959: 18-25). It seems as if cemeteries and mounds provided alternative burial modes in the late prehistoric-protohistoric. Earlier Oneota may have used mounds exclusively, since it represents a Woodland survival, but no evidence is yet available for the succession. Dispersal from the summer villages, either into *winter* villages or small *extended family encampments,* probably occurred to provide better foraging prospects and the small oval lodge type, common throughout the midwest, would be a convenient and snug shelter. Faunal analysis shows that the Lane Enclosure was occupied during the winter (Jenkins and Semken 1971MS), but the very fact that this site was apparently fortified suggests protection from enemy tribes was the overriding consideration. A basic hunting pattern of long trips in pursuit of bison seems likely although not yet confirmed by direct archaeological evidence. A short review of ethnological and historical accounts by Mildred Wedel (1961: 584-587) suggests organized summer buffalo hunts, but it is not known if they had the prolonged winter and summer hunts, such as occurred among the plains Indians.

The variety of potential Oneota sites—summer and winter villages, small winter camps, fortifications, food collecting camps, hunting camps, kill sites, rock shelter occupations, workshops, quarries, burial mounds, cemeteries, and petroglyph crevices—should not obscure the basic seasonal round. Oval and rectangular lodges, small varieties used in winter, and large ones for summer, were well adapted to climatic extremes in the midwest and constructed of materials close at hand. The figures 12 to 21 are photographs illustrating houses, materials, and construction techniques representative of tribes living within the woodlands, prairie, and plains. One of the more useful surveys of the literature is the monograph by David Bushnell, *Villages of the Algonquian, Siouan, and Caddoan Tribes West of the Mississippi,* published in 1922, and a number of sources for illustrations and description used in this chapter were located from his study. He is cited directly listing his sources because where these could be checked all were accurately quoted. In some cases he provides supplementary information such as identifying Joutel's visit to the Quapaw which is not immediately apparent in the original narrative. The only error found—one of omission— is the deletion of a sentence from Pike's description of the Osage houses where the explorer mentions that the bark lodges are unoccupied during the winter. In this instance I have directly cited the more recently edited narrative of Pike by Jackson to cover the omission.

The longhouse is distinctly different from the large but relatively narrow oval lodges generally considered typical of the midwest. The longhouse width, from 20 to 30 feet, could be sufficient for two families to live across from each other, a number of pairs extending the length of the house. The oval lodge, only half as wide, was more suitable for a single or an extended family group. Other longhouse characteristics include center posts and a ridge, structural necessities for large spans. The two main types of longhouses are the gable and the oval ended forms, although intermediate variations occur. A gable is the area of the front and back walls above the entryway, masking the ends of the roof that slope downward at an angle from a central ridge. The gable type construction usually has side walls. The second form with oval ends may lack side walls, or they may be present. It is usually characterized by curved arches, rather than a straight sloping roof. Either form may be covered with mats or bark, the gable type is generally bark and the oval curved arch type is mat covered. Both types have interior frames, but bark also required an outside frame to lash and hold the slabs together.

SIOUAN LANGUAGE GROUPS   The Oneota-Siouan correlation determined the selection of ethnographic examples. Table 4 provides a comparison of two classifications of Siouan languages derived from Wolff (1950) and Voegelin (1941). There is agreement on the major tribes, but the grouping of tribes into linguistic units presents some differences of opinion in part due to the definition of a language. Dhegiha is composed of four dialects: Omaha-Ponca, Osage, Kansa, and Quapaw. "Voegelin linked all four together and listed them as dialects of one language. While immediate mutual intelligibility may not actually exist between the members of this group, they seem so close linguistically that we may have a certain amount of neighbor intelligibility which may develop into mutual intelligibility after a short period of acquaintance between speakers of two different dialects." (Wolff 1950:64). Wolff's Group 1, Crow-Hidatsa, is composed of the two separated languages named after the tribes speaking them. Group 4 is composed of Oto-Missouri-Ioway, three dialects of a common language, Chiwere. Winnebago, a separate language from Chiwere, shows parallels in phonology and cognate words; the two languages are quite closely related. Group 3, Dakota, is a single language composed of separate dialects named after the tribes. Wolff's classification has historical implications: "On the basis of phonological and lexical similarities these languages may be grouped into seven distinct groups. . . . The assumption that these groups represent the first separations from the parent Proto-Siouan language, followed by later splits within each group, is implicit in the classification." (*Ibid.* 61).

The earlier Voegelin classification provides a larger grouping of possible linguistic relationships, dividing the Siouan languages into four major groups (table 4). The Eastern, Ohio Valley, and Missouri River groups are not relevant here. The Mississippi group contains five related languages representing a much larger number of tribes, but note his question marks relating Mandan, Dakota, and Dhegiha to the Chiwere-Winnebago. The Dakota language was spoken by the Teton, Yankton, and Assiniboin tribes who adapted to Missouri drainage bison hunting ecology prehistorically, and in some cases as a result of tribal pressures during the historic period. They and the Mandan provide no useful ethnographic examples of the huge mat and bark longhouses possibly built by their ancestors. The only Dakota exception is provided by the Santee, who originally built large bark houses.

Voegelin pointed out that the term Chiwere was used in various contexts to refer to (1) the single language spoken by the Ioway-Oto—Missouri, (2) the

Ioway-Oto-Missouri and the related Winnebago language, and (3) the "archaeologists' equation of Oneota, a cultural horizon, with an all too flexibly conceived
Chiwere group of languages." (1941: 249). He proposed dropping Chiwere as a
linguistic term, presenting it, somewhat tarnished, for the exclusive use of archaeologists. Wolff took the gift back and used it in his 1950 classification, because
it is simpler to refer to the Chiwere language rather than to the language spoken
by the Iowa-Oto-Missouri; but he uses the term in the restricted linguistic context.
Only a vague ethnographic hint appears of large houses among the Ioway, and
no mention can be found for the Oto and Missouri. These tribes were not well
described by the explorers and subsequently shifted tribal territories to the Missouri River plains environment during the time of the later American explorations.
The obsolete Winnebago longhouse was documented by Radin.

Dhegiha was spoken by a number of major tribes: Omaha-Ponca, Kansa,
Osage, and Quapaw. These tribes occupied various shifting territories along the
Mississippi Valley and its tributaries, and provide the clearest examples of houses
comparable to the Grant site. This does not imply that the builders of the Grant
village were Dhegiha rather than Chiwere speakers. Algonquian speaking tribes
such as the Sauk built large houses. Conceivably this structural form had a
long history in the Mississippi Valley, and is comparable to house types found in
the northeastern and southeastern regions of the United States. The early radiocarbon dates from the Grant site compared with the much later tribal distributions
of historic times make any but the most general linguistic association of dubious
value, and the problems can only be resolved by much more extensive archaeological investigations combined with additional linguistic evaluations of Siouan
relationships. If I were to hazard a guess at this time it would be to postulate
that longhouses were once widely used as summer dwellings by various Siouan
and other language groups in the Upper Mississippi Valley. However imprecise,
lexico-statistic dating of Siouan linguistic relationships would be most useful
in evaluating potential time depth of tribal relationships.

QUAPAW HOUSES   The Quapaw eventually settled west of the Mississippi
near the mouth of the Arkansas River. They are the southernmost of the Dhegiha
Siouan tribes, and their name signifies "downstream people" (Bushnell 1922: 108).
The Marquette—Joliet expedition visited the tribe in July 1673, noting "Their
cabins which are long and wide, are made of bark; they sleep at the two extremities,
which are raised about two feet from the ground." (*Ibid.* 108-9). The Joutel
narrative of the last La Salle expedition also mentions longhouses. On July 24,
1687 they arrived at four Quapaw villages. Joutel wrote:

> These Villages are built after a different Manner from the others we had seen
> before, in this Point, that the Cottages, which are alike as to their Materials and
> Rounding at the Top, are long, and cover'd with the Bark of Trees, and so very
> large, that several of them can hold two hundred Persons, belonging to several
> Families. The People are not so neat as the *Cenis* [Caddo], or the *Assonis* [Caddo],

in their Houses, for some of them lie on the Ground, without any Thing under them but some Mats, or dress'd Hide. How ever, some of them have more Conveniencies, but the Generality has not. All their Movables consist in some Earthen Vessels and oval wooden Platters, which are neatly made, and with which they drive a Trade. (*Ibid.* 109).

No later expedition mentions these large residences and they must have passed out of use among the Quapaw at an early period. The statement of "several families" suggests clan residences, although it would be useful to distinguish between the size of a house which could "hold" two hundred people at a ceremonial function and the number who lived in such a house as a residence.

THE OSAGE LONGHOUSE Zebulon Pike visited an Osage village in the Ozarks in August, 1806. In a supplement to his journal he wrote an excellent description of longhouse construction:

> The Osage lodges are generally constructed with upright posts, put firmly in the ground, of about 20 feet in height, with a crotch at the top; they are generally about 12 feet distant from each other; in the crotch of those posts, are put the ridge poles, over which are bent small poles, the end of which are brought down and fastened to a row of stakes of about 5 feet in height; these stakes are fastened together with three horizontal bars, and from [form] the flank walls of the lodge. The gable ends are generally broad slabs and rounded off to the ridge pole. The whole of the building and sides are covered with matting made of rushes, of two or three feet in length, and four feet in width, which are joined together, and entirely exclude the rain. The doors are in the side of the building, and generally are one on each side. The fires are made in holes in the center of the lodge; the smoke ascending through apertures left in the roof for the purpose; at one end of the dwelling is a raised platform, about three feet from the ground, which is covered with bear skins, and generally holds all the choice furniture of the master, and on which repose his honorable guests.
>
> In fact with neatness and a pleasing companion, they would compose a very comfortable and pleasant summer habitation, but are left in the winter for the woods; they vary in length from 36 to 100 feet. (Jackson 1966, vol. 2: 31-32).

No width dimensions are given, but from the height of twenty feet and allowing for curvature of the roof they may have been some twenty-five feet wide. The length dimensions of up to one hundred feet fits closely with the Grant data. A much smaller Osage house frame built in the same way as those described by Pike appears in figure 12. It has a ridge pole, resting on support posts. The lodges were so closely spaced, it was sometimes difficult to pass between them, a settlement pattern also reported for the Kansa.

KANSA LONGHOUSES In the summer of 1811, Major George Sibley described a Kansa town in his journal. It was a large flourishing place, located in present day Kansas:

> The Konsee town is seated immediately on the north bank of the Konsee River, about one hundred miles by its course above its junction with the Missouri; in a beautiful prairie of moderate extent, which is nearly encircled by the River; one of its Northern branches (commonly called the Republican fork, which falls in a few hundred paces above the village) and a small creek that flows into the north branch. On the north and southwest it is overhung by a

chain of high prairie hills which give a very pleasing effect to the whole scene.

The town contains one hundred and twenty-eight houses or lodges which are generally about 60 feet long and 25 feet wide, constructed of stout poles and saplings arranged in form of an arbour and covered with skins, bark and mats; they are commodious and quite comfortable. The place for fire is simply a hole in the earth, under the ridge pole of the roof, where an opening is left for the smoke to pass off. All the larger lodges have two, sometimes three, fire places; one for each family dwelling in it. The town is built without much regard to order; there are no regular streets or avenues. The lodges are erected pretty compactly together in crooked rows, allowing barely space sufficient to admit a man to pass between them. The avenues between these crooked rows are kept in tolerable decent order and the village is on the whole rather neat and cleanly than otherwise. Their little fields or patches of corn, beans and pumpkins, which they had just finished planting, and which constitute their whole variety, are seen in various directions, at convenient distances around the village. (Sibley manuscript quoted by Bushnell 1922: 90).

This village may actually have been near present day Manhattan, Kansas (Waldo Wedel 1959: 52). The Sibley manuscript is in *Nebraska Historical Publications* 1922 vol. 20: 5-11, but the above passage on pages 5-6 lacks the fireplace description and shows other minor differences, suggesting an inexact copy, and for this reason we have followed Bushnell's extract. After the Louisiana Purchase a treaty was supposedly made with Kansa living at the mouth of the Saline River, but this is mentioned in a later report by McGee (1897: 193), and is not confirmed by other documents (Waldo Wedel 1959: 52). The McGee report, *if accurate,* suggests lineage residential groups, for it mentions some 1,500 Indians living in 30 lodges; and this would average 50 per house. The village seen by Sibley had more than four times as many structures, many occupied by two or three families, however these may be defined. If this latter village had 300 nuclear families living in 128 lodges, the total population might also approximate 1,500 people, but an average of only 12 per house. The Kansa lived west of the Missouri for a long time, and both historic and prehistoric sites attributed to this tribe have earth lodges in addition to undefined structures (Wedel 1959: 59, 128, 135, 171, 190). From other accounts the Kansa lived in small skin covered lodges when the band dispersed for the winter foraging, and used different types of houses, including a round bark or thatched structure with a sunken floor and internal supports patterned after the typical earth lodge (figure 21).

OMAHA AND PONCA   The Dhegiha Ponca and Omaha spoke the same language with minor vocabulary differences and lived in earth lodges and tipis within the Missouri drainage. The Omaha said they once lived in bark houses (Fletcher 1911: 78). The Ponca had four types of dwellings at the time of white contact; the round earth lodge, the tipi, a circular lodge more often covered with hides than bark, and an elongated lodge. The housing reflects their mixed Woodland-Prairie-Plains orientation (Howard 1965: 56-60). One of Howard's informants described the round lodge being made "by taking long green poles, sticking them into the ground, and bending them over and tying them at the top. Other poles or vines were tied around (horizontally) to make the framework. The whole thing was then covered with hides." The long lodge "was made in the same way but was as much as forty feet long one way." (*Ibid.* 57). The absence of a central ridge pole and internal supports from the description suggests that the Ponca longhouse was a simplified version compared with those made by the other Dhegiha tribes.

IOWAY, OTO, AND MISSOURI   The Chiwere language (excluding Winnebago) is not clearly correlated with the Siouan longhouse, in part I think, because of the lack of early French descriptions. The Ioway told Skinner that they had built a number of different house forms including the plains earth lodge, wattle and daub rectangular houses, tipis and bark and mat covered lodges. The bark house was rectangular, twenty by forty feet. Their small oval houses covered by mats or bark measured ten feet wide and fourteen to twenty feet long with internal wall benches and a central fireplace. Skinner reports he could not obtain any information on seasonal use of these structures but thought it probable that the Ioway had lived in the small oval houses during the winter and used the large bark houses during the summer in the same fashion as the Central Algonquians (1926: 271-277). The photograph of an Ioway oval lodge is from Kansas and is typical, although somewhat untidy, with the traditional exterior framework consolidating the bark slabs (figure 16). Samuel M. Irvin, a missionary among the Ioway for twenty-six years beginning in 1837 wrote, "They were a wild, warlike, roving people, and in a most wretched condition, depending mainly on the chase for a subsistence. Their habitations were of the most frail and temporary kind. There were shelters in the form of huts or houses made of the bark of trees stretched over slender poles and tied together with bark strings, or they were tents or lodges made of the skins of the buffalo or elk, and sewed together with the sinews of these animals. These bark houses were mainly for summer shelter, and would in a few years yield to the wear of time, when they would be abandoned and a new location sought. The skin tents were carried with them, and made their habitations wherever they chanced to stop. They were strictly a migratory and unsettled people." (Plank 1908: 312). Skinner was apparently unaware of this missionary's report on the seasonal use of winter tipis and summer oval bark lodges. The only historical account mentioning the use of large houses is the statement by Maximilian in April 1833 while traveling in an area occupied by Ioways. "The canal between Nadaway Island and the cantonment is called Nadaway Slew, at the end of which we saw the remains of some Indian huts. In a dark glen in the forest, we observed a long Indian hut, which occupied almost its whole breadth, and must have served for a great number of persons." (Maximilian 1843: 124 quoted by Bushnell 1922: 114). The long lodge may have been ceremonial rather than a residence.

Oto and Missouri   The Oto had adapted themselves to a plains environment by the time of the early nineteenth century explorations and during the summer lived in substantial earth lodges. Their winter tipis were covered with bison hides. A third type of Oto dwelling was small lodges covered with thick oak bark, a seeming survival from the Mississippi forested environment. No adequate ethnological account of the Missouri house types exists (see Bushnell 1922: 114-121).

THE WINNEBAGO TEN-FIRE LODGE   The migration legends of the Ioway, Oto, and Missouri state they lived with the Winnebago and then moved westward (Griffin 1937: 181). Ioway chiefs told Dorsey that "their people and the Oto, Missouri, Omaha, and Ponca 'once formed part of the Winnebago nation.' According to the traditions of these tribes, at an early period they came with the Winnebago from their priscan home north of the Great Lakes, but that the Winnebago stopped on the shore of a great lake (Lake Michigan), attracted by the abundant fish." The dominant, but apparently dubious Winnebago tradition is their origin at Green Bay. The historical legends are described by Radin (1923: 49ff.) who is cautious about their value. He presents the separate and fragmentary mythological explanations describing how various groups left the Winnebago: first the Quapaw, followed by the Missouri, and Ioway. One of Radin's informants said: "Four lodges once left the main tribe at Prairie du Chien. . . .Some people believe that the Oto are this lost branch, for they speak the same language with but few differences and use many old words that the Winnebago employed long ago but have now given up." (*Ibid.* 51). The subject of Siouan origin myths and migrations is fraught with difficulties. Despite this, the reciprocal supporting traditions of related tribes puts the Winnebago in a central role; for they remained in the Mississippi riverine environment.

The description of the ten-fire lodge shows some of the same basic features variously reported for Quapaw, Osage, and Kansa: ridge poles, central supports, separate standing wall posts connected to roof arches, a special platform at the rear, and sleeping platforms along the sides. The arch poles were straight rather than curved.

> According to the oldest informants, the earliest type of lodge used by the Winnebago was the ten-fire gable lodge, of which there were two types, rectangular in form, one built on a platform and the other on the ground. Poles of cedar, forked at the top, formed the sides. Through the forks transverse poles laid to which the gable roof was attached. Three poles * were arranged in the center of the lodge for the better support of the roof. Beds were placed along both of the long sides on a platform raised 2 feet * . Frequently a platform 4 to 5 feet high was erected in the rear of the lodge and partitioned off. Here the favorite child of the family lived when he was fasting. In front of the lodge a spot was always kept carefully cleared * . There were two doorways to the lodge. Often the entrances were shaded with boughs. According to some informants, this was only done for the chief's lodge. According to another description of the gable lodge, there were only two central poles, one at each entrance; these were always painted blue to symbolize the day.
>
> As far as can be learned at the present time, the platform lodges were merely gable lodges on platforms. What purpose the platform served is now difficult to determine, but most Winnebago questioned said that it was provided as a protection against the dampness of the ground and insects.
>
> The ceremonial lodge was merely a large, long bark lodge. The grass lodge seems to have been a roughly constructed round lodge with a covering of grass instead of bark. The sweat lodge was a round bark lodge having a framework of four poles. The tipi was of a simple type provided with a three-pole framework.

> All the evidence obtained points to the fact that lodges of these types were used synchronously. According to the myths and the oldest informants, in ancient times a village occupied for a considerable period consisted entirely of gable lodges, but these seem to have given way to the round and long type, probably borrowed from the Central Algonquian. The gable type seems to have held its own, however, among the more western villages of the Winnebago. The round bark lodges were used in winter and the reed matting lodges in spring and summer. In the spring those who still lived in bark lodges covered the roofs with reed matting, as that material shed water more effectually than bark. The tipi was generally used on the hunt, the grass lodge merely for a shelter overnight.
> All the duties connected with the construction of the lodge belonged to the woman. These duties do not seem to have been restricted to any special class of women except in the construction of ceremonial lodges, in which only women who had passed their climacteric could participate. (Radin 1923: 104-106. * indicates deleted native words).

The ten-fire lodge would be most substantial to judge from Iroquois structures. There is some debate on the question, but Lloyd's annotated edition of Morgan seems convincing that each partitioned segment of the Iroquois longhouse held two families, one on each side of the central passageway, and they shared a common fireplace (Morgan 1954, vol. 2: 287-301). The traditional ten-fire lodge of the Winnebago, if residential, could have contained twenty families, or on the average, about one hundred people. Depending on the size of family compartments—the Iroquois descriptions vary—a five-fire Iroquois residence would be one hundred and twenty feet long. A ten-fire Winnebago lodge with compartments twelve feet long, half a common Iroquois length, would have at least attained the same length. The ceremonial lodges of the Iroquois had many more fireplaces than the residential longhouses and this suggests that the Winnebago ten-fire lodge was for the same purpose, their residential lodges having fewer hearths.

The difference between the platform and gable lodges was puzzling to Radin, his informants being vague on this point. Rather than a house on a raised platform suggested by Radin, the difference might have been one of internal platform arrangement. The use of a high end platform in addition to side platforms resembles the Osage description. The Iroquois had a special ceremonial longhouse which may provide another analogous form. It was partly residential but had some special features, and is described in the annotated edition of Morgan. It is derived from an analysis of Bartram's description, based on his visit to the Onondaga in 1743 and a visit to the Huron by a Frenchman a century earlier:

> Bartram and his party were ambassadors, and so were quartered not in an ordinary dwelling but in the council-house, which was especially arranged for the accommodation of visitors and for feasts and assemblies. Such use being but temporary, the apartments were small, like those in a summer hotel, and each apartment consisted, as Bartram describes it, and as his plan plainly indicates, of a single bunk, five by seven, in which he and his two companions could lie comfortably or 'set before the fire,' for there was a fire between each pair of opposite apartments in this house as in others. Over these bunks was the platform where they placed their goods. It was, moreover, necessary to reduce the span of this platform in a council-house, because of the great weight

which might come upon it. The short distance between the fires was also a con-
venience during councils. Light is thrown on this subject from a curious source.
In September, 1637, there was brought to the Huron village of Tondakhra an
Iroquois prisoner named Saouandanoncoua, who was tortured in the war
council-house. This house must have been about the size of Bartram's, for it
contained eleven fires six feet apart, and up and down the house through and
around these fires Saouandanoncoua was driven till he dropped, while the
old men watched the entertainment from their places above 'upon a sort of
platform which runs on each side the entire length of the cabins, while the
young men were below, but so crowded that they were, so to speak, on top of
each other, until there was scarcely passage along the fires'. . . .It is possible
that an unusual number of fires may have been lighted for this entertainment,
but the probabilities are the other way. (Morgan 1954, vol. 2: 297).

The council house of one Huron leader was named "the house of the cut-off
heads." (Kinetz 1965: 41).

DAKOTA SANTEE   The various tribes of the Dakota linguistic stock adopted
horse nomadism on the plains in historic times, although most of them may
have originally had a forest-prairie adapted technology. Dakota migrations are a
very complex subject, and this review is limited to Santee houses in villages
seen by American explorers along the Mississippi in present day Minnesota. The
Santee remained in the Mississippi Valley; Schoolcraft visited one settlement
August 2, 1820:

Here is a Sioux band of twelve lodges, and consisting of about two hundred
souls, who plant corn upon the adjoining plain, and cultivate the cucumber,
and pumpkin. They sallied from their lodges on seeing us approach, and
gathering upon the bank of the river fired a kind of *feu-de-joie,* and manifested
the utmost satisfaction in our landing. . .We were conducted into his cabin
which is spacious, being about sixty feet in length by thirty in width—built
in a permanent manner of logs, [*i.e.* substantial poles] and covered with bark.
(Schoolcraft 1821: 317-318, cited in Bushnell 1922:49).

Some thirty years later the bark lodges were smaller, following the historic
trend observed among other Siouan groups. In May, 1849, E.S. Seymour described Little Crow's village Kaposia, in present day St. Paul.

During the time I visited them, the Indians were living in skin lodges [tipis],
such as they use during the winter, and when traveling. These are formed of
long, slender poles, stuck in the ground, in a circle of about eight feet in diameter, and united at the top, and covered with the raw hide of the buffalo,
having the hair scraped off. They are in the form of a cone, and can be distinguished from those of the Winnebagos and other Indians as far as they can
be seen. During the summer they live in bark houses, which are more spacious,
and when seen from a distance, resemble, in form and appearance, the log
cabins of the whites. When passing in sight of the village, a few days after-
ward, I noticed that they had removed their skin lodges, and erected their
bark houses. The population of this village, as I before remarked, is from
250 to 300 souls. (Seymour 1850: 137-138, cited in Bushnell 1922:50).

Bushnell shows two illustrations of the Dakota bark houses (our figure 18)
dating from 1850 and 1851 when the houses were smaller than they were

earlier. The village of Kaposia is additionally described:

> the lodges are from eight to fifteen feet in diameter, about ten to fifteen
> feet high and made of buffalo-skins tanned. Elk skins are used for
> this purpose also. The summer house is built of wood, or perches set upright,
> twenty or thirty feet long, by fifteen or twenty wide. The perches are set in
> the ground about one foot, and are about six feet out of the ground. Over
> this is put a roof of elm bark. They are very comfortable for summer use.
> The lodge of skin lasts three or four years; the lodge of wood seven or eight
> years. (Prescott *in* Schoolcraft 1857, vol. 4: 67, cited in Bushnell 1922:51).

The description of the Santee bark houses in the northern Mississippi Valley
reflects a pattern found intermittently south to the Quapaws. The Santee had
the side upright poles, center posts, and originally the size, of the summer houses
used elsewhere over this wide area.

4. ETHNOGRAPHY: CONSTRUCTION OF BARK AND MAT LODGES

A number of aboriginal house types occurred in the Northern Mississippi Valley. The wattle and daub house of Middle Mississippian cultural origins, sporadic in occurrence, never became the dominant form, and even Aztalan shows that other types occur (Wittry and Baerreis 1958). The use of tipis, common in historic times, may have gained popularity with the availability of the horse travois to draw them. Because of the weight of individual hides, some fifty pounds, they were originally skewered rather than sewn, for easy separation when backpacked during the communal hunts out on the prairies. An occasional hide might be lashed over a bark or mat house to stop a leak in the same way that pieces of canvas were later used for the same purpose. There are a few references to hide covers on large houses but the examples are well west of the Mississippi; among the Ponca and Kansa during the nineteenth century. No ethnographic or historical references describe earth lodges occurring within the Northern Mississippi Valley, the nearest prehistoric examples so far found in Iowa being at the Wittrock site of Mill Creek culture, on a tributary of the Little Sioux River, nearly two-hundred-fifty airline miles from the nearest point on the Mississippi. We may anticipate that a few isolated examples of this dominant village type of the Missouri will be found much further eastwards, as more prehistoric structures are excavated. If present, they never became dominant because earth covered roofs were less well adapted than bark or mats to the higher rainfall of the Mississippi drainage. The pioneer sod houses and roofed dugouts were sometimes built where logs were scarce and before sawmills and railroad transportation provided cheap lumber for cabins. The pioneers seldom built such sod houses in the eastern counties of Iowa, showing a historic parallel with prehistoric distributions.

In prehistoric times mat and bark covered lodges provided the basic aboriginal housing from the Northern Mississippi Valley eastwards past the Great Lakes to the Atlantic Coast. The materials were efficient and durable. The Santee living on the Mississippi above the present Minnesota line told Prescott that their elk and bison tipi covers lasted three or four years; their bark houses lasted seven or eight years. However, the proper preparation of bark required spring cutting and a subsequent curing period, so that its use in house construction needed considerable forethought and planning. Rushes and reeds also required preparation before they could be bound into house mats. The Winnebago according to Radin's account in the preceding chapter lived under bark in the winter and reeds during the summer. Their bark construction was not completely watertight and if they did not move into a new reed house at the end of winter, they covered their old bark house with reed mats. Properly built, elm and other deciduous tree bark could be made waterproof, and served as summer house covers for a number of tribes. I am unaware of any single account which discusses the details of lodge construction and have written the following description from an archaeological point of view.

THE INTERIOR POLE FRAME   The basic interior house frame is illustrated by three examples in figures 12 and 13. In its simplest form, pairs of slender poles were set in the ground, bent over and tied, forming arches strengthened and kept in place by lashing horizontal trusses which formed the side walls and roof. Among the Winnebago the arch poles were ironwood "driven into the ground" and tied together with basswood bark (Radin 1923: 104). Similarly arch poles were "forced" into the ground by the Ojibwa, while the Ponca made arches by "sticking them into ground". (Bushnell 1922: 13 and Howard 1965: 57). Even the Santee with larger houses only set wall posts one foot deep (Prescott in Schoolcraft 1857, vol. 4: 67). The Huron and Ottawa at Mackinac according to the account by Cadillac written towards the end of the seventeenth century "drive poles as thick as one's leg and very long into the ground, and join them to one another by making them curve and bend over at the top, and then by fastening them together with whitewood bark. . ." (Kinietz 1965: 41). Despite the weight of all this description it is difficult to conceive of large house posts being driven into the ground.

All three illustrations of interior frames show the horizontal wall struts lashed in place outside the arches. A closer look at the Ojibwa framework shows that three poles form each arch, the two wall posts bound together by a third top member overlapping each side for a considerable extent. The Sauk and Fox arch is formed by a simple pair of overlapping poles. The Osage arches were not bound to each other in a simple overlapping curve but were lashed to the ridge pole forming a more pointed roof.

The Osage framework shows the use of three internal support posts, in the example shown, one post at each end of the lodge. The central ridge pole carries the thrust of the roof downwards rather than diagonally outwards, and smaller braces bind the internal support posts to the whole framework, forming a flexible but integral structural unit. The Fox structure shows that very insubstantial and crude post framing could support the mat house covering, and the Ojibwa frame shows that smaller three part arches do not require internal supports. This strongly suggests that the Osage house frame was built more strongly than necessary; a cultural survival in construction from the time when Osage houses were the much larger longhouses described by Zebulon Pike.

The interior frame of the Grant site houses had interior posts, probably on the order of twenty feet high, with forked ends supporting a central ridge made of a series of small lashed poles. Parallels with historic structures among the Winnebago, Osage, and Santee, suggest that the Grant side walls were formed of posts rising five or six feet out of the ground. The long roof poles were lashed top and bottom, to ridge and wall. Such huge arches, twenty feet high and twenty-four to thirty feet across, even with internal trusses, exerted substantial lateral pressure outwards. If simply forced into the ground at shallow depths, the wall butts would have worked loose endangering the structure. The archaeological evidence shows pointed post holes up to thirty inches in depth, too deep for posts to be driven. The women may have scooped out the greater part of each hole with a convenient tool such as a clam shell. Limestone rocks brought into the site were commonly found in both humus and subsoil beside post holes to strengthen the set of the post in the sandy soil.

BARK PREPARATION   Coniferous forests provided birch bark sheets and when the band moved these were sometimes removed from the houses, rolled up, and reused. Catlin describes Ojibwa portaging birch bark house covers and their other possessions around St. Anthony Falls at present day Minneapolis (1841, vol. 1: 138). They sewed small pieces of birch bark into large sheets, twenty by three feet wide in size, which were easily carried when rolled (Kinietz 1965: 325). In deciduous forests bark from a number of trees proved suitable, probably depending upon what was readily available. Elm bark was widely used from New York State through the Mississippi Valley. Most references are vague on tree species, but specific citations include the use of red elm and ash bark by the Iroquois, ash, elm, fir, spruce and cedar by the Huron, cedar by the Winnebago, walnut and elm by the Ioway, oak among the Oto, poplar bark by the Kansa, and scattered references to the use of elm by the Ojibwa, Santee, and Sauk and Fox. (The above references in order of occurrence are Morgan 1954, vol. 1: 309, Kinietz 1965: 40, Radin 1923: 104, Skinner 1926: 276, and Bushnell 1922: 120, 95, 77, 51, and 39).

Bark used in house construction required advance preparation. The Ioway peeled walnut or elm bark in the spring of the year and stacked it in piles six feet high, each layer of bark separated by poles allowing it to air. It reportedly took two years for the bark to season properly before it could be used in house construction (Skinner 1926: 276). A similar description of bark preparation is contained in the account by the Frenchman Lafitaux describing the Iroquois.

> The pieces of bark are prepared a long time before using. They are removed from the trees, after girdling, when the sap is rising, because then they are more easily stripped off; and after the outer surface, which is too knotty, has been removed from them, they pile them compactly one on the other that they may not warp, and thus they are left to dry. The poles and the wood necessary in building the structure are prepared in the same way, and when the time has come to commence work, the youth of the village, for whose encouragement a feast has been provided, are invited, and in a day or two all the work is set up, more from the multitude of hands working upon it than by the diligence of the workers. (Morgan 1954, vol. 2: 289).

The rough side of the bark was often left on rather than being skinned off. This can be seen in the illustrations of bark on Sauk and Fox, Winnebago, Ioway, Santee, and Kansa lodges. I know of no examples of skinned bark being used in the midwest.

COVERING THE BARK HOUSE   The flattened bark slabs were irregular in
shape; the Iroquois slabs were fifteen inches wide and six feet long, clapboarded,
an upper course overlapping part of the next lower. Where edges of two bark
boards on the same course met, they were overlapped like shingles to provide a
weathertight covering. The Iroquois laid the grain of the bark horizontally on
the house sides and ends. Roof slabs were laid with the grain running down for
better drainage. Morgan states that the boards were stitched through and through
with fastenings. Skinner's Ioway informants said that the roof poles were notched
to provide places to tie on the bark. Such lashing points would of course be a
useful detail to keep the bark slabs from slipping. Bark grain and pitch of wall
determined the slab position, an obvious necessity since moisture collecting in
corrugations caused bark rot, which led to continual repairs. The small oval structures of the Winnebago and Ojibwa, and the larger Kansa house all show the slabs
tied vertically. The larger gabled houses had horizontally positioned slabs on the
upright ends and house sides where drainage was unimportant.

MATS FOR HOUSE COVERINGS   Mats were made of rushes or reeds bound
together in flat sheets (figure 13). Other illustrations show that the mats were
placed with the reeds perpendicular to the ground to shed water more effectively.
Mats were only waterproof when fastened to the inner framework in overlapping
layers; particularly on the roof. Bark seems to have been the traditional covering
for most of the longhouses, but the Osage were a major exception. Their house
mats were two or three feet in length, and four feet wide. In terms of seasonal
construction it is revealing to note that mat preparation usually took place in
the fall of the year, hardly a propitious time to build summer houses. The description of mat preparation practiced by the Man or Human clan of the Prairie
Potawatomi shows that it could be accompanied by considerable ritual:

> The women of the tribe, in general, may not cut rushes for this purpose with-
> out the consent of the wife of the chief of the local band, or of the tribe, as the
> case may be. In the fall when the rushes are ripe for cutting, the chief's wife is
> notified that the women wish to proceed to the marshes. She makes a feast to
> which they are invited, tells them that they may go, and takes the lead herself.
>   Once arrived at the shore of the lake or marsh they encamp in a row, and no
> one may approach the water until permitted. A spring is located to supply water
> for drinking and cooking, and, at the request of a female messenger from the
> chief's wife, all begin to cook and prepare a feast, while the men go hunting for
> game.
>   The chief woman goes to the bank of the lake alone with tobacco, and prays
> to the lake, her clan ancestors, the water, and the earth. She faces the east and
> prays to the manitou of that quarter, then to the south, then to the west, and
> last of all to the north, where she prays to the god of cold. She tells the powers
> of the four quarters that she and her women are about to cut rushes, then enters
> the water and cuts four herself. When she returns with these the women cut the
> rushes and bring them ashore and tie them in bundles. A woman who is under-
> going her periodical sickness is not permitted to enter the water, but must, as

usual, camp apart, while others do her work for her.

The rushes are stood up in bundles on the south side of each wigwam, between two upright poles placed there to support them. They are guarded by
a rope stretched around to prevent anyone from coming near. Next morning
all the women heat water, and, taking a bundle at a time, scald the end to the
depth of the kettle. Then they are tied at the top and bottom and put away
in a clean place. When the sun is bright they are untied and spread out to
bleach, after which they are sorted, the two center shoots from each package
being set aside to make a certain cover mat. When the sorted bundles are tied
up again, five or six rushes from each are tied up separately.

When all is in readiness, each woman who wishes to start her mats, sends
invitation sticks to four or five women of her acquaintance, asking each to
come at a certain time, and bring her *magwe*, or long, flat, curving needle of
deer rib. The rushes are spread on the ground, touching each other laterally,
in the shape of the mat, and the women commence to sew them together
with their needles and twisted fibre twine. Each woman is required to sew
four times the length of a rush but most stay to finish at least one mat. Two
mats are considered a day's work.

When all the mats are sewed, a certain day is appointed for cutting lodge
poles. When these are gathered, trimmed and peeled so that they will not
wear or tear a hole in the lodge mats, the wigwam frames are put up. Then
another day is appointed for covering the lodges. . . .

When all the mats have been made, a feast of thanksgiving is held before
they can be used, either as floor or wall coverings. The chief is called in,
and he prays and harangues his audience on the subject of women as home
makers. He is given a mat as a fee, and it is considered an honor for a woman
to be able to say that the chief has received a mat from her and uses it in
his wigwam. Sometimes, if the chief is not available, some distinguished
Brave is called upon to perform this rite.

Bone awls were once used, and locust thorns served the same purpose.
Holes were burned in the latter to fit them for use as needles. The crooked
bone of the raccoon was also used as an awl. Long, flat, curving mat needles
were made of deer ribs. These had a central perforation. (Skinner 1926a:
291-294).

EXTERIOR FRAMEWORK   After the bark was lashed to the interior framework, an exterior set of poles consolidated the slabs. The Winnebago almost
duplicated the inner framework on the outside to secure the bark. From Radin's
description it appears that there were outside arches tied to the corresponding
inner arches, the lashing passing through the bark sheath. The exterior horizontal
struts were secured by wedging them underneath the exterior arch poles. These
struts were not lashed to inner supports or even to the arches themselves on
smaller Winnebago houses (figure 15). The struts on the larger Kansa houses
vary; they wedged small sticks underneath the exterior frame, but lashed
larger horizontal poles outside the arches (figure 20). Some of the illustrated
bark lodges show an exterior strut tied along the bases of the outside arches. This
would cut down on drafts between the ground and bark edge.

The round and the long bark lodges are constructed in a very simple
manner. These are built of poles of ironwood * driven into the ground,
bent over and lashed to other poles which meet them from the opposite
direction. The poles are tied together with basswood bark*. The same
material is used in attaching to these poles the cedar bark that forms the

walls of the lodge. The walls are supported on the inside by a varying number
of poles * attached to the corresponding poles of the other side. In many cases
a series of transverse poles * are inserted beneath the exterior vertical poles. . . .
The bark roofs are incased in frames made of irregularly distributed vertical poles
with generally one transverse pole. If the roofs are of reed matting two or three
of the external poles have poles attached to them which are arched across the
matting. The reed matting lodges, as a rule, have no external vertical poles and
only two transverse poles each, one on the outside and one on the inside. (Radin
1923: 104. *Indicates native words given in the text. References to his illustrations are omitted).

Well preserved archaeological post patterns may reflect the use of bark sheaths if
double inner-outer posts are observed, separated only by the thickness of the bark.
The absence of the outside framework for reed matting may well apply to the
large prehistoric lodges. Yet even among the small Winnebago structures some
exceptions occur, as can be seen in figure 15 upper, identified by Radin perhaps
incorrectly as a mat covered lodge which has the double or exterior frame. The
double framed bark lodge, recovered in mats could even result in a third frame.
Seasonal repairs would thus result in accumulations of layers and arch poles and
this is clearly what was being done when one examines some prehistoric post hole
patterns closely.

PORCHES Open-sided, flat-roofed porches were often built to extend the effective living space of the lodge during the summer. They were built of stout supports,
selected with a fork at the tip which held the horizontal roof poles. The illustration shows these roof supports were thicker than the bent arch poles used in the
lodge itself. Bark sheets, mats, or hides covered the flat roofs, covering which was
held down by other poles. The purpose of the porches was to provide shade as
well as a summer cooking area outside the lodge itself, and the roof did not need
to be watertight and almost certainly was not. Several illustrations show these
structures in various stages of repair (figures 14, 16, 17). The Ojibwa also built
these shelters and such structures occur throughout most of North America.

Particular attention is called to the rare double Winnebago lodge connected
by a common porch shelter (figure 14). Excavating the remains of a comparable
prehistoric structure would provide a post pattern resembling a longhouse. The
porch poles are larger and the spacing is farther apart than the lodge walls, and
the entire length of post holes would probably not align well. If one examines
the illustrations of the other porch structures the post patterns do not coincide
with the lodge walls, suggesting that it would not be difficult to differentiate the
porches from lodges in archaeological excavations.

STORAGE AND INTERIOR DESIGN Pits used for food storage occur with
associated house patterns throughout the midwest. At the Grant site many pits
lie at or outside the wall lines, and those within the houses are very few considering
the number of occupants. There is no clear association of any one of the storage
pits with any particular house. For example, a storage pit within the south end

of House 1 might actually be associated with House 3, having been carefully placed outside that structure after the House 1 site was no longer in use. A few charred corn kernels appear in a number of storage pits. One would suspect that corn filled pits would more frequently occur at the winter camps, built in the fall of the year after the harvests. Pit storage was an obvious precaution for groups living in flammable bark houses as their food reserves might easily be destroyed. This need is clearly stated by Sagard who visited the Huron for ten months during 1623 to 1624.

> For fear of fire, to which they are subject, they often put whatever they have that is most precious into vats and bury them in deep holes dug in their cabins and then cover them with the same earth; this gives protection not only from fire but also from the hands of thieves, for they have no other chest nor closet in all their household but these little casks. (Kinietz 1965: 40).

The internal design of the small bark lodges was very simple; a doorway in one end gave access to the interior with a central fireplace, and benches for sitting and sleeping built around the sides. The interior of the more ancient longhouses is very problematical. The main entry could have been at the sides rather than at the ends: figures 14 and 17 provide later ethnographic examples among the Winnebago, and Pike's account gives an earlier description of this design. On the other hand, the Santee doorway was on the gabled end of their bark lodges. Inside the doorway, there may have been a simple partitioned vestibule, with a long narrow passageway set lengthwise through the center of the house. The central support posts every twelve feet in the Osage longhouses would provide a place to lash internal support beams or poles running horizontally across the house, forming A-frames. Such beams with a few uprights, would provide convenient partitions when hung with mats, providing some privacy for the sleeping benches. Shelves for storage could easily be built above the bunks and all the personal and household belongings; bows and arrows, robes, wooden bowls, medicine bundles, and other possessions would be tied or hung from the walls. In the first account of a Huron longhouse, Champlain wrote in 1615 that in winter the Indians slept on mats beside the fire. "On both sides is a sort of platform, four feet in height, on which they sleep in summer to escape the annoyance of fleas of which they have many. . . ." (Kinietz 1965: 39).

The occurrence of various longhouse forms in the southeastern United States lies beyond the scope of this report. Driver and Massey (1957), Driver (1969), Willey (1966), Jennings (1968) provide some summary information on ethnology and archaeological sequences.

5. INTERPRETATION: THE GRANT SUMMER VILLAGE

The diversion into historical and ethnographic sources provides a background for fuller evaluation of archaeological evidence. Excavations in New York and elsewhere show longhouse post patterns surprisingly similar to those of the Grant site in Iowa. One example, a section of the Bates site plan drawn by Ritchie (1965: 285) is a superimposed house pattern comparable in length, width, rounded ends, and internal features to Grant Houses 1 to 7 illustrated in figure 7. If one examines the Bates plan closely there are repeated pairs of double posts suggesting the presence of an interior and exterior frame characteristic of bark house sheathing.

The Anker and Oak Forest sites of the Oneota Tradition south of Chicago provide examples geographically closer, but physically smaller (Bluhm *et al.* 1961). The Oak Forest village plan is compared with the Grant site in figure 24, the illustrations all being redrawn to the same scale. Dimensions of all the houses were previously given in table 3. The houses from Illinois are, on the average, half the width and length of the Grant houses, and cover only a quarter to less than half of the floor area but otherwise are structurally similar. Two floor plans of the post pattern of the Illinois houses appear in figure 22 redrawn to the same scale, omitting the distinction between deep and shallow posts, and certain other information. Interpreting the factual data from the two publications by Bluhm in the light of additional research now allows somewhat expanded conclusions.

The subject of seasonal occupation of the two Illinois sites was not discussed in the original reports although one has an illustration of a winter house. Historic and ethnographic evidence throughout most of the Upper Mississippi Valley repeatedly describes seasonal settlements, particularly small camps during the winter and larger summer houses. The midwestern occupation of the longhouses is thus, apparently, strikingly dissimilar from the various Iroquoian longhouse settlements in the Great Lakes area and central New York, which were yearly residences when visited by the explorers. The reason for shifting into small winter homes is obvious; the high roofed longhouses were almost impossible to heat during the formidable, cold weather common in the midwest. Lafitau who had stayed in an Iroquois longhouse vividly described the cold weather problem:

> They double their doors to protect themselves from the cold and smoke; and make what seems like a second door with blankets of skins or wool. In the common and ordinary cold weather, their cabins are sufficiently warm, but when the northwest winds blow and there occurs one of those severe Canadian spells which last seven and eight days in succession, and are cold enough to split stones, then the cold having penetrated in, I cannot understand how they can endure it, being as little covered as they are, especially those who sleep far from the fire. (Morgan 1954, vol. 2: 292).

The Indians could spend winters in such houses, as the Iroquois example shows, but it does not seem to represent the traditional midwestern pattern.

Summer occupation of the Oak Forest and Anker villages is supported by an evaluation of the faunal remains listed in their reports, identified by Paul Parmalee of the Illinois State Museum. Table 6 lists the birds identified from the two sites and I have added the time of year each species was in the Mississippi Valley during the late nineteenth century based on information taken from Cooke (1888). There are reports of these birds which are exceptions to the migration times, and the Mississippi flyway of Illinois is slightly different from the Lake Michigan area around Chicago. Nevertheless a number of these birds are migratory and provide an excellent estimate of average hunting months. At the Anker site the mallard might have been hunted as late as early January when it left the area; the Canada goose arriving in early February. However, these are exceptional cases, and the lesser scaup and wood duck are clearly absent during the winter. The only time when all four birds could be hunted is from middle March to middle September, and if they did not manage to shoot the first arrivals and tardy departures, a village occupation from April to September is suggested, corresponding to the ethnographic pattern.

The Oak Forest site shows a closer range of migrations, the widest range represented by the green winged teal from early March to early November. The wild turkey is present the year round, as is the bald eagle on occasion. Yet the presence of the sandhill crane and passenger pigeon suggests that all of the birds were hunted during April to September. Both sites show a potentially similar range of available months for bird hunting despite the fact that different birds were present in the small sample. Given a seasonal occupation there is no likelihood that the season was winter.

The Anker house was originally identified as a probably ceremonial lodge because of its size, a natural conclusion with no prior archaeological information to interpret. Half the width of the Grant houses and somewhat shorter, this house is definitely smaller than many longhouses inhabited by various tribes during the period of discovery. One would be hard pressed in the light of ethnographic evidence to identify all of the Grant houses as ceremonial lodges, since extensive trenching showed no smaller residential houses within the village. Internal support posts are present in all nine Oak Forest and Anker houses although it would be desirable for more than two of the nine house plans to be published, considering the unprecedented nature of the discoveries. The internal support posts identify all the houses as having ridge poles, the type of construction common in the Mississippi Valley but uncommon in the small wickiups.

The post patterns suggest these Illinois houses were repeatedly refurbished and rebuilt during the spring of the year when the band returned to summer quarters. The Oak Forest house appears to show a double interior and exterior framework of arch poles which may indicate bark sheathing. The lengthwise spacing of the posts is closer than a single house construction would require. The otherwise redundant center posts also suggest several major rebuildings and additional patching. The more densely grouped post holes of the Anker house

walls and its redundant internal supports provide evidence of successive rebuildings and three changes in house size. If bark lasts seven or eight years,
the Anker cluster of house posts might indicate four or five major rebuildings,
various other repairs, and a periodic seasonal reoccupation of perhaps as long as
half a century. These houses must have presented a variegated appearance during
the last stages of occupation: the house sheath having an accretion of several
layers of bark, extra house posts jammed beneath the ridge to support a sagging
frame, and probably mats and extra bark sheets of different species covering the
most conspicuous leaks. Finally, we can imagine, the Indians reluctantly concluded that the houses were uninhabitable after many years of patching and
shoring up; and they built new houses salvaging such materials as they could
from the abandoned buildings. Flecks of charcoal in some of the post holes
suggest that fire finally terminated the life of some structures.

GRANT POST HOLES The Grant post patterns do not clearly indicate the type
of house cover. It is most unlikely that hides covered most of the framework
because (1) there are no ethnological parallels in the Mississippi Valley, (2) faunal
identifications show that bison were not hunted in the immediate vicinity of the
site, and (3) it would require an enormous number of hides of bison, elk or deer
in an area where massive hunting for large game cannot be clearly documented
by faunal remains. The evaluation of whether mat or bark sheathing was used
rests upon the identification of double frame construction from the post patterns.
The house wall in the east house area, figure 11, apparently has a double pattern.
The inspection of wall lines in the west house area shows numerous double
posts and irregularities which can be interpreted as an exterior frame. There are
also considerable lengths of post walls that appear to be isolated single lines. The
evidence is equivocal, but it is possible that many of the exterior wall posts were
shallow in depth and small in diameter, leaving inconspicuous pointed depressions
in the subsoil that may have been missed. The outside posts were nonstructural,
their purpose being to hold the bark against the larger inner posts which bore the
weight of the building.

The faunal evidence of summer occupation is less favorable for interpretation. The few bone remains were identified by Holmes A. Semken, vertebrate
paleontologist with the University of Iowa Geology Department (Appendix).
The sample did not lend itself to a qualitative evaluation of the mammal bones
by sex and age of the species.

GRANT HOUSES ABOVE THE POST MOLDS The appearance of the Grant
houses can be inferred from similar structures described and drawn in historic
times within the Mississippi Valley. There are two main possibilities: (1) a
gable frame with side wall poles and roof eaves, or (2) a rounded roof built by
bending single poles to the ridge. Either one could be covered with mats or bark.
The appearance of both possible houses of Grant site dimensions was sketched

under my direction by Frank Sindelar, Graphic Arts, The University of Iowa (figures 25, 26). Both were drawn to the Grant site floor dimensions of House 2, sixty-four feet long by twenty feet high, twenty-six feet wide with curving ends and show House 6 in the background in its actual position.

The drawing of the gabled longhouse roofed with bark was based on the following information. The side walls follow the Osage example described by Zebulon Pike, and the descriptions of the Santee lodges. The illustrations by Seth Eastman (figure 18), and F.B. Mayer (in Bushnell 1922 plate 21) were followed. The Sauk bark covered structures were also used, particularly the fully sheathed house which has somewhat rounded ends (figure 19 upper). Although the early Osage houses were mat covered, this house is bark covered with the typical double frame. Bark summer houses were most commonly reported for the Santee, Sauk and Fox, Winnebago gable lodges, Ioway, Kansa, Quapaw, and apparently the Omaha-Ponca. It is conceivable that the information Radin recorded of mat-covered summer houses is not the result of a long tradition, but rather a shift because of the decline of bark technology in house construction among the Winnebago during the nineteenth century. The height of the ridge pole is twenty feet, the only clear statement of this house dimension appearing in Pike. The Sauk and Santee illustrations show that even small houses were proportionally tall, twelve to fifteen feet to the ridge—estimated from the various illustrations. An Iroquois longhouse was twenty or more feet high. The doorways are located in the ends of the houses providing direct access to the lengthwise passageway, a position repeatedly shown in the illustrations. Only the Osage and Winnebago lodges had doorways in the sides.

The other artist's reconstruction, figure 26, has curved arches, lacking side walls. The Iroquois made both curved and straight roofed houses. The curved type provides historical continuity with the smaller arch construction commonly built throughout historic times. The illustration shows mat covering to provide a contrasting example with the exterior bark framework. The doorways have been placed at the side following the Osage placement and the houses are really no more than an enlargement of the mat covered Winnebago house shown in figure 17. All things considered, I prefer the bark covered, gable house reconstruction of the Grant house type.

VILLAGE PLAN   The village plan can be inferred from the excavations although a number of doubtful points require large scale excavations for resolution. The settlement pattern of the village, figure 23, was drawn from the excavation plan figure 5, and the letters and numbers indicate points requiring explanation or evaluation. Houses 2 and 6 were excavated and they are identified in figure 7. House 8, incompletely located is known only from the west wall. The east wall posts were apparently obscured by storage pits, since we did not have enough time to extend the trenches and locate the ends of the house (figure 11). The House 8 location could be shifted north along its wall lines, and it was placed

in its suggested position in order to avoid as much of the mound as possible.
(D) This fourth house labeled (?) is projected from 8, paralleling the relationship of houses 2 and 6. It seems likely that at least one house was situated in
the north part of the village to complete the grouping around the central area.
It may be noted, however, that the partial house cluster at the Oak Forest site
is incomplete (figure 24).

The present-day outline of the linear mound is indicated by the dash outline, reduced in height and spread by plowing. Its aboriginal dimensions are
approximated by the solid line centered within the present perimeter. The old
excavation trench X-X appeared in both of our transverse trenches, but the position of this disturbance is west of the linear mound midline. If the lengthwise
position of the linear mound is shifted ten feet west, instead of being centrally
placed within the spread out mound remnants, it would be clear of the storage
pits we found in its east side. In such a reconstructed position it would have
formed a prominent western boundary of the village.

The round mound by House 8 is similarly reconstructed in outline from its
present flattened, widened perimeter. It contained probable Woodland burials
within the center of the house floor and the house itself is clearly intrusive.
Barely visible today, aboriginally the mound may have been low and inconspicuous.
It is puzzling that the house is located over the mound. If it had been built slightly
east, the mound could have easily been avoided. One explanation which could be
tested by excavation is that the house was smaller and south of the mound. Later
extensions of the house following the original wall lines found the mound in the
way and simply cut into it.

The A trench on the excavation plan located no houses and very few storage
pits. Two small pits occurred in the square west of the linear mound indicative
of some storage outside the main limits of the village. The approximate village
boundary is supported by the following evidence. The east side marks the last
storage pit, no others occurring in the B trench beyond that point towards the
ravine. The west side of the village boundary is drawn through the three test
trenches which had a few sherds and one storage pit. The test trenches parallel to
it on the south, and the north-south test trench had no evidence of Oneota occupation. Storage pits in the A and B trenches stop near the edge of the linear
mound as shown. The north edge of the village boundary is problematical, but
could not be much larger because the terrace edge falls steeply away on two sides.
The village center had no houses and only three storage pits occurred in the excavated trench across it. The village boundary thus represents the occupied area
defined by storage pits where this information could be determined. The settlement pattern at the Grant site is very different from the extensive village sites
previously reported from the Upper Iowa Valley and elsewhere. In some, but not
in all cases, these larger sites may well represent repeated occupations by different
groups of Oneota people over a much longer period of time than the Grant site
duration. Closer definitions of the ceramic distributions at the larger sites, group-

ing related storage pits, and comparing them with the contents of other pits, will probably show horizontal stratigraphy at those extensively occupied localities. The Grant village was a small compact area about one acre in extent. It is suggestive that the Oneota Lane Enclosure on the same terrace is comparable in size, and that the Late Woodland Hartley Fort is even smaller. There is no suggestion of a stockade at the Grant village, although trenches crossed the periphery of occupation in order to locate these post molds had they been present.

POPULATION ESTIMATE   The well defined east-west perimeters of the village show several large houses grouped around a village center. The village undoubtedly fluctuated in size. Some summers only one house might be occupied; with crowding as many as six houses could have jammed together within the village limits. Both Pike for the Osage and Sibley's description of Kansa longhouses described them as crowded together with barely enough room for a man to pass between; and this indicates village space could be densely settled on occasion. The village population also changed during the course of each summer; many of the more active men were away on combined hunting and war party forays. The scarcity of animal bone suggests hunting and butchering was carried out some distance from the village. Meat rather than the carcass was brought back. There exists the greatest disparity between the small number of game animals represented in the village refuse and substantial numbers of human occupants. The Appendix by Semken identifies animal species and the number of individuals represented. To summarize: the Grant fauna includes eight fish, three turtles, one snake, several birds, one shrew, one beaver, one lemming, one mouse, one wapiti (the archaeologists's elk), four deer and three domestic dogs. Usable meat weights for an elk, deer, and beaver are respectively 350, 100, and 38.5 pounds (White 1954). If the dogs, turtles and fish add another 60 pounds of usable meat, the potential food from identified animals is only 850 pounds, or less than half a ton. This is enough to provide a good sized Indian band with picnic lunches, but it is obviously insufficient to sustain them year after year at the Grant site.

The village refuse thus provides no basis for estimating the Grant population because they were not throwing significant amounts of trash into their emptied storage pits. There may be an undiscovered refuse dump near the village, perhaps over the edge of the terrace. The virtual absence of trash in the storage pits also emphasizes the economic importance of gathering wild foods and harvesting domesticated corn and other plants.

A settlement pattern can provide a population estimate derived from the approximate number of Indians living in each house multiplied by the number of houses occupied at the same time. From prehistoric evidence, several interpretations can be equally supported. If we are prepared to assume that the village settlement pattern with four houses (figure 23) is a reasonable average, we can approximately calculate the band size from the archaeological evidence of

structures. The floor plan of the houses is problematical but using Iroquois examples it consisted of partitioned residential areas along the sides fronting on the
common passageway down the center. Pike's statement of central support posts
every twelve feet may be taken as an average width of each family area. A sixty-
five foot longhouse at the Grant site potentially could have five compartments
on each side, housing ten nuclear families. Living space would be adequate. The
average Grant longhouse is at least twenty-four feet wide, allowing a four foot
passageway. Each family's room open at the front and partitioned at the sides
would have two sleeping benches end-to-end along the wall. These could be six
feet long and five feet wide, sufficient for an Indian couple and their children.
This allows five feet between the berths and passageway. There would be room
enough to stand up and turn around without being seen by every other family
in the longhouse, except of course, for the immediate neighbors living across
the unscreened passageway, with whom one also shared the intimacies of a fireplace.

The estimate of a four house summer village, some ten families in each,
yields a base estimate of forty nuclear families, or two hundred people; a reasonable size. Some Santee summer villages farther up the Mississippi had populations
of about this size in historic times.

House width dimensions at the Grant site are quite similar, ranging in
various structures from twenty-two to thirty feet, but most are about twenty-
five feet. The most conspicuous dimensional variation is length. Not only do
the lengths of individual houses vary, but the rebuildings of a single structure
show variations in length. The explorers also reported that lengths of building
varied within a single village. The stability of width as opposed to length strongly suggests that the central passageway and residential areas were standardized.
The most obvious explanation for house size variation would then be the number
of families requiring shelter. Changes in length can be explained if residential kin
groups such as clans occupied each house. The requirements of the house clans
would vary within the village and also over time.

6. TECHNOLOGY: DESCRIPTION OF ARTIFACTS

The sparse remains of pottery and other artifacts probably reflect the technological emphasis on perishable materials—bark, wood, reeds, leather, sinew, feathers, and other kinds of animal and vegetable derived products which have disappeared.

SHAPED STONE *Abrading* tools were used for sanding, polishing, and sharpening. Three broken specimens of sandstone are customarily identified as *arrowshaft sanders* or polishers (figure 28B). The groove depth is less than half of the width since this type was apparently used in pairs. Groove size ranges from 0.61 to 0.87 cm wide and 1.5 to 2.9 cm deep. One specimen shows secondary use for sharpening a thin edged tool, the wear appearing as a narrow groove on the reverse side. The *sharpening stone* or abrader (figure 27E) shows random striations to a depth of 0.40 cm which are less rounded and closer to a V-shape in cross section compared with the arrowshaft sanders. This tool would be useful for sharpening bone implements and grinding the edges of hafted flaked stone tools. The *wide grooved* specimen has a shallow but wide depression and could have been used for sharpening or shaping bone. The material is dolomitic limestone rather than sandstone. The groove measures 2.24 cm wide and 0.32 cm deep.

Grinding artifacts include a fragmentary *mano* and *metate,* presumably used for preparing corn meal (figure 27B, G). The small thin *grinding slab* seems to have had a discoidal shape, and its original function is unknown. It could have been used for preparing paint pigment. It is only 1.1 cm thick.

Hammering tools are consistently rare at Allamakee County Oneota sites (table 7). The *celt* is a unique example found while clearing House 6, trench G, and is located on the plan (figure 5). Made from fieldstone and shaped by pecking, it is quite crude in appearance. Measuring 16.1 cm long, 4.7 cm wide, and 2.05 cm thick, the largely missing butt end shows battering, and the front edge is ground sharp on both faces. The usage marks are suggestive of a chisel function for this celt. It is very puzzling why there is a virtual absence of large wood-working tools made from shaped stone at Oneota sites. The extensive use of poles and bark in house construction, general woodcraft, and firewood gathering would make large tools indispensable, or so one might think.

Pipes and *tablets* are extremely rare. The New Albin inscribed tablet first reported by Orr (1922) lacked clear excavation provenience, being found while digging a cellar. It was made from catlinite and shows Middle Mississippian cultural associations in design motifs like a number of others reported elsewhere in the midwest (Bray 1963). Orr himself found no carved tablets in any of his Oneota excavations. The small carved limestone specimen from the Grant site is the first specimen of its type found in an Upper Iowa excavation which can

46

be documented. Too small for a tablet, it might more properly be termed a charm such as might be carried in a medicine bag. It is triangular in shape, unworked on two edges, and the third edge has five notches (figure 29B). On both sides appears a lightly grooved V-shaped decoration. The stone appears to be a small natural pebble which was slightly modified. The decoration motif is of extreme importance for it resembles the so-called "turkey track" petroglyph identified by Orr at a number of Upper Iowa rock crevices. Orr considered that these petroglyphs dated from the Woodland occupations, but restudy suggests that the rock was too soft to preserve petroglyphs of that antiquity. This charm from storage pit 13 in the west house area is clearly supporting evidence for linking the petroglyph motif with Oneota culture, and by association provides a radiocarbon dated context for a number of otherwise undated and undateable crevices which have no cultural material but the petroglyphs themselves (McKusick 1971a).

Miscellaneous objects include an unpolished *stone ball* (figure 29E) 2.62 cm in diameter, and a *grooved ornament* made from quartz* (figure 29C). The latter has a maximum diameter of 1.50 cm and a maximum thickness of 1.34 cm. This specimen came from storage pit 13 where the other carved charm was found. The *natural concavity* (figure 27A) is not an artifact since there is no evidence of modification. It was associated with burial B and appears to be a Woodland secondary burial of two individuals in the linear mound 14 (figure 46 lower).

OTHER MATERIALS The *bison scapula* hoe (figure 27D) from storage pit 39 shows a typical removal of the *spina scapulae*. It is the only evidence of bison from the site. The *human cranium* may have been part of a large pendant, but no worked edge is present. The hole 4.3 mm in diameter has no beveled edges. One *worked antler tip* (resembling figure 28A) does not show a finished artifact form. The curved *os penis* or *baculum* of the racoon *Procyon lotor* shows sharpening and acquired high polish from use. Its artifactual purpose is unknown. Thus human, bison and racoon sources for bone artifacts occur, but are not present in the unmodified bone from the refuse. The *notched shell* (figure 28G) is the only artifact of this material which can be identified. The illustration does not show the interior of the notch which does have a flattened, weathered surface and not a fresh break. The *copper ornament* (figure 29F) is made from a rolled sheet.

The site area had obviously intrusive *iron*, including a harrow tooth and five nails. No brass trade goods, beads, bottle glass, or sheet iron, or nonaboriginal ceramics, appeared in the collections. The site was remarkably free of recent debris. Three small fragments of clay daub were found in the west house area. The daub (figure 29E) has impressions of fine sticks or thatch. Daub has not been previously reported from Oneota sites in this area. It was too rare at the Grant site to be a building material, but might have been used mixed with grass to plug annoying holes in bark house sheathing.

*See note page 90 describing specimen.

FLAKED STONE   The chert chipping waste suggests that percussion flakes used for smaller artifacts were struck off from prepared striking platforms. The material appears to be locally available white chert. Brown chalcedony (Knife River flint) from western North Dakota is sometimes present in Woodland Tradition sites in Allamakee County, but this trade was apparently broken off in later times and no examples of this material are present in either the Grant or Lane Enclosure collections. Similarly, Sioux Quartzite and obsidian rarely and sporadically occur in eastern Iowa at Middle Woodland mound sites but are absent later. The absence of catlinite originating from southwestern Minnesota is similarly suggestive of a Mississippi River orientation with little meaningful contact with the Missouri drainage. Catlinite does occur at some northeast Oneota sites, but with extreme rarity. The only carving present in the Grant collections is made on limestone; a substitute or less desirable material.

  Projectile points were uncommon, 6 of 10 examples being fragmentary. The usual thin, triangular variety occurred with either a straight or slightly concave base (figure 31). The side-notched triangular point associated with Middle Mississippian culture is entirely absent. The size of the four complete triangular points expressed in the range from smallest to largest is: base 13.6 to 15.8 mm, length 14.8 to 23.2 mm, and thickness 3.3 to 4.2 mm. The fragmentary points were somewhat larger. The three larger hafted points (figure 28) are apparently associated with the Oneota occupation. Specimens D and E came from storage pit 26 which had Grant Oneota pottery. Specimen C was found while clearing a post hole in the west house area, southeast part of section D. These three examples could be hafted knives, souvenir Woodland points, or much less likely accidentally displaced from the Woodland mounds into a seemingly Oneota context.

  Bifacially flaked edges occur on various artifact groups, for the most part classified as knives. Trianguloid knives (figure 33C, E) resemble large triangular projectiles. Three show no marginal retouch, are crudely flaked, with a maximum thickness from 9.4 to 12.3 mm which clearly puts them outside the thin triangular projectile point group. Three others are thinner 4.8 to 7.2 mm, with retouched edges, and one of them would almost be a small projectile except for its irregular triangular shape. The size range between the largest and smallest trianguloid knife is: length 23.6 to 42.4, and base 20.1 to 22.6 mm. As a group these are crude and small, not comparable to the large brown chalcedony knife Mildred Wedel (1959: 49) used as the example of this type. The latter specimen from the New Galena Mound Group is a most atypical material from Upper Iowa Oneota sites. The single *ellipsoidal knife* (figure 28F) is 2.6 wide, 6.8 long and 1.1 cm thick, somewhat irregular in shape, and not comparable in workmanship to those commonly found as grave goods. *Curved flake* knives are crude, only 2 of 5 showing any secondary flaking and this is restricted to one short edge. They resemble several crudely fashioned triangular knives in craftsmanship, in that they appear to be shaped by percussion flaking, leaving a strong but irregular edge. Three *scraper knives* are large, thick flakes, irregularly shaped (figure 30D) with a minimal preparation of a worked edge including secondary flaking or use flake marks. The seven blade fragments appear to be segments of small ellipsoidal or triangular knives.

Unifacial scrapers are a common artifact, and various types occur. The *ridged end scrapers* have a steeply worked face, and commonly contract to a pointed butt (figure 32G, H), but others are more crudely shaped (figure 32F). As a group the face length and vertical face height ranges are respectively from 16.5 to 19.5, and 7.1 to 11.2 mm. *Flat end scrapers* are made from a flake which shows little ridge trimming. The example illustrated (figure 32L) has some upper flaking but the maximum specimen thickness is only 3.8 mm, about half of the ridged type. *Flake end scrapers* are crude, and the large specimen (figure 30H) lacks marginal retouch. Others are too irregular to be either flat or ridged varieties and seem to be made from random small flakes with irregular retouch (figure 32K). Some *round scrapers* have been termed "thumb nail" because of their size, and are common at Oneota sites. They are shaped from round to irregular flat flakes with one steeply flaked working edge (figure 32A-E). *Side scrapers* show a long worked edge, which may be curved, straight or irregular. Four of 11 examples show two worked sides, being double side scrapers (figure 33A, B, D, F). There is an overlapping function on one specimen which could equally be classified as an end scraper (figure 33D). *Flake scrapers* are random spalls lacking marginal retouch, but have what appear to be use flakes on one naturally sharp edge.

Pointed flaked stone tools often termed drills could be used for boring, punching and engraving. Both shape and flaking characteristics are variable in this group. The large thick spall (figure 30C) has been modified to form a sharp point. Three small drills have slightly expanded bases (figure 31C, F), the latter being a broken tip. The bi-pointed specimen has both tips broken (figure 31B) but is neatly flaked along the shaft and can be identified with some assurance. It may be noted that Mildred Wedel illustrates four gravers, including among them a specimen comparable to our group of expanded base drills (see 1959 figure 5E, second specimen from left).

Two crudely flaked, thick specimens have a triangular shape and may be termed *core choppers* (figure 30A, B). They are grouped under bifacial flaked artifacts although they are not knives.

In table 7 the artifact inventory is compared with specimens listed in Mildred Wedel (1959 table 1) by both type and frequency. The inventory representative of the Orr Focus contains 398 specimens from the various Upper Iowa sites excavated by Keyes and Orr. The Grant sample totaling 103 artifacts is only one-fourth the size. There is a broad comparability of types in all categories except copper, trade iron, and glass; some absences and differential frequencies being anticipated in comparing samples. The tabulation obscures one important comparison. The 1930s excavations were much more selective in artifact collection, discarding worked flakes and some of the cruder artifact forms which are identified in the Grant collection. Had these been available the Orr Focus collections would have been substantially larger.

POTTERY Despite substantial excavations the sherd sample from the Grant site was extremely low, in marked contrast to the abundant and large sherds from the Lane Enclosure. The analysis of the Grant pottery is complete, but its significant features can be best described in comparison with the later pottery. The total Grant sample includes 91 rims and handles, 296 decorated body and 787 plain body, many of small size. A comparative sample of 200 rims provides a perspective of Lane Enclosure tempering, profiles, line thickness, punctate patterns, and rim thickness measurements. The lip decoration traits were based on a sample of 400 Lane Enclosure rims.

Leaching As a result of relative age and local soil conditions, shell tempering in the paste disintegrates, leaving irregular angular holes on the surface. Examining the exterior sherd surfaces, *no leaching* occurs when all exposed shell is intact. *Medium leaching* results in a mixture of surface shell and angular pits, and *extreme leaching* has little or no surface shell. Anticipating soil conditions to be nearly equivalent between two sites, the much greater percentage of leached Grant sherds appears to be the result of greater age (table 8). Perhaps as a result of leaching Grant pottery also appears to be softer, more friable, and less compacted. While this characteristic may not be present at other Grant site components, the early dates suggest it may be a significant trait, since radiocarbon chronology shows that Grant pottery has twice the relative age of sherds representative of the Lane Enclosure. Systematic pH tests should be taken at future Oneota excavations in this area, combined with the leaching index used here.

Trailed lines Measurements show a significant increased popularity of narrow lines in the later pottery. It may be noted that the rim and body decorations are frequently made with the same tool, and consequently there is a consistent trend of broader lip notching associated with the medium lines on Grant pottery.

Punctates A distinctive distribution appears in punctate patterns, the Grant examples occurring as a row or fringe appended to line patterns while Lane Enclosure examples fill triangular areas or bands. In the two samples the distinction is absolute. Larger samples will probably show some examples of each type, but the preponderance of one or the other should prove to be a useful distinguishing characteristic. The size is a second punctate trait which separates the pottery, Grant examples being larger, and duplicated in our experiments with an antler tip. Lane Enclosure specimens are often smaller, frequently suggesting a sharp pointed bone awl. Punctate size is a reflection of other decoration techniques, the somewhat blunt antler commonly being used on Grant pottery for lines, rim notch, and punctate, while sharper, thinner tools produced much of the characteristic Lane Enclosure decoration. Variations in form occur with the angle and characteristics of the tool. The description of Missouri Oneota pottery by Henning (1970) defines three groups of punctates; those made with (1) a sharp point tool, (2) a round medium tool, and (3) finger or thumb impressions. The tool or finger may be vertical to the surface or pressed in at the angle leaving elongate marks. Punctates rarely decorate Grant pottery, and no examples of finger punctates occur. Medium elongate punctates occur 13 times, and medium vertical punctates appear once. Another sherd has sharp pointed punctates, set in two parallel rows. One sherd decorated with oblique lines contains short dash lines superficially resembling punctates.

Lane Enclosure sherds may have occasional punctate rows but none of these occur in the rim sample described here. Medium tool punctates made with a vertically held tool occur on 4 sherds, and elongate examples appear on three others. Sharp pointed tool punctates made with a vertical tool appear 3 times and there are 6 examples of the elongate form. One sherd has dash lines resembling punctates. Comparing the two groups, finger pressed punctates do not appear in either, and the pointed tool examples are more numerous at the Lane Enclosure, which is also conspicuous for the filled areas.

Rim measurements   Sherd edges show that the flaring rims in both groups were made by doubling over the clay sheet. This was done by extending the vessel wall up twice the desired rim height, and folding it back over. The fold left an interior separation line, imperfectly joined, which can be seen on the broken edges of a number of the rims. This technique explains the greater rim thickness compared with the body of the vessel. Profiles suggest a slightly more graceful, flowing shape for Lane Enclosure rims (figure 43) although this is extremely difficult to confirm by measurements. Grant rim height percentages show a greater emphasis on low rim and fewer tall rims. The rim thickness measurements taken at lip, midpoint and bend of rim are not distinctive between the two samples.

Vessel shape   All Grant rims can be identified as parts of flared rim containers. Ceramic forms absent include straight rim jars, bottles, miniature pots, pottery pipes, and figurine fragments. The Lane Enclosure sample is more variable, some 3% of the containers lack flared rims. Among 200 large rim sherds examined, there is one bottle and 5 straight sided jars, apparently round bottomed. The bottle and a jar sherd have rounded lips approaching a rolled rim, the remaining jar sherds (two from the same container) have a flattened lip. No other ceramic forms were observed.

Handles   Nineteen handles, fragments, and attachments show a predominance of broad straps, 2.5 to 4 cm wide, commonly concave on the inner surface. Seven straps are too incomplete for measurement or decoration traits, and five are plain. Three are decorated with vertical, broad trailed lines, and one other has a single finger pressed punctate. Only three loop handles occur, 15% of the small sample, ranging in width from 0.8 to 2 cm. The narrowest has been flattened, having three finger notches on the handle ridge; the other two handles being plain. All nine handles with the rim lip intact show the typical finger notches observed on the other rims.

Fifty Lane Enclosure handles include 44 broad to medium straps and 6 loops, a distribution comparable with the Grant collection. Straps vary from 1.7 to 5.3 cm wide, 20 specimens being undecorated, 3 indeterminate, 2 decorated with horizontal rows of sharp punctates, and 19 having a vertical, broad trailed decoration of one or more lines. Loops include 2 undecorated, one pressed to form a vertical ridge, and two flattened sides with finger tip impressions. Decoration of the rim lip, most commonly with a finger tip, is present on all specimens but one, which is plain above the point of handle attachment.

The two Oneota handle samples do not differ substantially. Loops are a minority, with the flattened, finger decorated type present, and the straps are similar. The point of upper handle attachment sometimes meets at the rim and sometimes below it. Lane Enclosure has the rare presence of narrow lines and sharp punctates, traits absent in the Grant collection.

Rim decoration   Differences in kind and frequency of rim decoration appear to show the most diagnostic and easily identified traits distinguishing various midwestern Oneota groups. A recent study of three Missouri sites by Henning (1970) defines eight categories of rim lip decoration and his classification was subsequently applied by Straffin (1971) to the closely similar pottery from the Kingston site in southeast Iowa. This classification is difficult to apply to the Orr and Grant pottery despite Henning's inclusion of a separate category for finger tip impressions. After practicing on clay with various stone and bone tools, it became apparent that it was extremely difficult to distinguish between finger and tool impressions. Most of the Lane Enclosure decoration could be duplicated with a deer bone awl using the point for fine punctates, slash marks and narrow lines. The area near the tip duplicated narrow notches, and the wider segment could make wedge-like marks; the latter also being made by finger tips. In contrast, the Grant pottery decoration was more closely duplicated by a blunter antler tip for the medium lines, notches, and punctates. With both groups very broad trailed lines, which are not common, were apparently finger trailing. Wide notches could be made with either an antler tool or a finger.

Comparisons between Grant and Lane Enclosure rim decoration traits confirm the general impression of broader decorative elements on Grant pottery (table 8). There are also differences in the kinds of lip decoration present (figures 34, 53, 54). Flattened marks are broad and intermittent on otherwise plain lips. Rare, and only found on Lane Enclosure pottery, it is possible these are not intentional decoration marks but were left while the pot was resting upside down before firing. *Narrow notches,* ranging from shallow, indistinct marks to deeper cuts account for one-fourth of Lane Enclosure pottery; a decoration trait totally lacking in Grant pottery. *Wedge notches* overlap *medium notches* in width, the difference between them being shape. The wedges are almost always irregular. Characteristically the V-shape is vertical on one side, broadly sloping on the other, and often there is a fine line at the joint which could be duplicated by either a flattened awl or fingernail. This prominent characteristic is almost absent on Grant pottery but commonly used on the later pottery. Almost 70% of Grant rims have *medium notch* lip decoration and it tends to be wider than that on Lane Enclosure pottery. *Interior notching,* both vertical and oblique tool marks, is relatively more common on Grant rims. These listed comparisons do not include another conspicuous trait. A minority of Lane Enclosure notches are *intermittent groups* alternating with plain rim areas. This trait does not appear on Grant pottery, but is partially reflected in the absence of plain rim sherds compared with the presence of plain rims on the later pottery.

THE GRANT TYPE   Diagnostic ceramic traits distinguish the Grant pottery type from other known Oneota groups based on a small sample of decorated rims and bodysherds. In summary, the predominant vessel shape is medium sized containers with loop or strap handles attached to outflaring rims. Rims are high, relative to most Oneota pottery. They are thickened by doubling over the clay sheet. Plain, undecorated rims are rare, the majority (67% of the sample) having uninterrupted medium notches, the wide notches and interior tool marks being the other two major rim decoration forms. Punctates are medium to large, and trailed lines tend to be of medium (3 to 3.5 mm) width. Design motifs stress parallel lines in triangular or vertical patterns with border punctate rows. Zones of punctates or dash marks and curvilinear lines are absent. The sample has a high percentage of heavily leached surface shell temper (78%) although shell remains in the sherd centers. It is not known whether this will be a diagnostic trait at other components having the Grant type, although it may be since the relative age of the pottery is substantial.

The Grant type is a local variety dating from about A.D. 1000 and the assignment of other components will broaden the presently known characteristics. The diagnostic criteria are most clearly seen when contrasting the group with later Lane Enclosure pottery, a dated A.D. 1450-1700 member of the Allamakee Trailed type. Lane Enclosure rims are somewhat higher on the average, and emphasize traits not present on Grant rims such as narrow and wedge notching comprising half the sample. Interrupted rim decoration is present. Decorative lines are narrower, and punctates or dash lines form zones of triangles or bands. The surface shell is much less weathered being largely intact on 70% of the sample. Because of weathering it is difficult to reconstruct the paste characteristics of Grant pottery. It appears to be softer, more friable, and less well compacted than the later pottery. Some characteristics are shared between the two types although it is presently difficult to gauge the significance of these potential continuities. Both groups of pottery have similar rim profiles, handle construction, and some similar decorative techniques particularly the medium notching and possibly some line motifs. Curvilinear lines are absent in both groups.

7. CONCLUSIONS

Very serious problems occur when one attempts to correlate the explorers' descriptions of longhouses with the structures reported by archaeological investigators. The search for house types is just beginning in some areas, data are often inadequate, and the variety of housing used during the seasonal round of subsistence activity provides further complications. Nevertheless, one would expect closer correlations than in fact seem to occur, a circumstance which raises doubts and necessary reservations about generalizations concerning the Oneota-Siouan association with longhouses, territorial limits of occurrence, time depth, and potential origin, or origins of this structural type within the Mississippi Valley.

WISCONSIN One of the house types reported for the Ioway by Skinner (1926) was rectangular in shape, with upright wall posts chinked with daub, and roofed with sod. This ethnological example was used by Griffin (1960: 818-819) to illustrate the more substantial types of dwellings he predicted would be found associated with the Lake Winnebago Focus in Wisconsin and the early Oneota Aspect as a group. Confirming evidence seemed to be present; a small sub-rectangular house had been found at the Oneota Carcajou Point site, the wall posts being set in a builders trench. Griffin suggested that the wattle and daub house types were probably present as far north as the Cambria village in Minnesota, a site which is not Oneota, but illustrates one geographical dimension of Middle Mississippian influences. Some variability was present at Carcajou Point when Hall subsequently published his plans; one series of incompletely excavated post holes representing a rather small but amorphous structure, and another unidentified structural post line similarly lacked a wall trench (Hall 1962, vol. 2, plates 3 and 4). Nevertheless, these other incomplete structures can be variously interpreted as supplementary or seasonal dwellings. Carcajou Point remains a crucial example disputing the suggested longhouse distributions because part of the sequence is a component of the Lake Koshkonong Focus, dating from about A.D. 1000, being contemporaneous with the Grant village. Concerning the house sequence problem Hall (1962, vol. 1: 95-96) concluded,

> At first glance there is little resemblance between house types suggested for the early and late periods at Carcajou. The similarity of Category C houses to Middle Mississippi varieties has been mentioned, and those of Category B have been compared to the gabled summer lodge of historic Wisconsin tribes. It bears repeating, however, that no evidence of either clay daub or wattle was found nor any clear examples of excavated house floors. Category C construction was in this sense typologically intermediate between that of the semisubterranean wattle and daub houses of the type known in Wisconsin as Aztalan and that of dwellings of Category B, which were built on the surface and probably covered with bark. [Hall's footnote: For a description of houses excavated at Aztalan by the Wisconsin Archae-

ological Survey see Wittry and Baerreis 1958. In his original excavations at
Aztalan, S.A. Barrett discovered two houses which he reported as such (1933:
162-64, 175), but the presence of others may be inferred from such evidence as
a subsurface house floor and fired clay hearth described as Barrett's Feature
IV-50 (159-63).] This comparison is not intended to illustrate a developmental
sequence, because Category B houses undoubtedly have a long history and there
is a great variety in domestic architecture even at Aztalan. It is meant only to
point out that the difference between houses of Categories B and C was in great
part stylistic. There is no evidence at the Carcajou site of a shift from proper
pit houses to surface structures or from wattle and daub cover to bark or mats,
although such a change may have taken place within the history of the local
group before their settlement of Lake Koshkonong.

The report by Peske (1966) substantiates the presence of aboriginal garden beds
at a probable Oneota summer village, but furnishes no information on the village
houses, and the thorough and interesting review of the historical development of
Oneota theories and relationships in Wisconsin by Gibbon (1970) does not
emphasize structural evidence. McKern, Ritzenthaler and others conceived of
Oneota villages as fairly permanent settlements on high river or lake beaches
and the eastern groups may have used perishable "pole and bark houses."
(Gibbon 1970: 288).

The Wisconsin Middle Mississippian site of Aztalan bears a much less crucial
role to the development of Oneota than was once believed. Various theories prior
to the mid-1960s placed an emphasis on Oneota development from Old Village
Middle Mississippian origins late in time. Griffin reviewing the evidence before
Oneota radiocarbon dates became available in quantity suggested that the climate
deteriorated around A.D. 1300-1650, affecting Mississippian Pattern agricultural
practices. This led him to suggest that Oneota developed directly from an expanding Middle Mississippian culture which was subjected to increased climatic
change in its northernmost outposts (Griffin 1961, reviewed in Gibbon 1970:
289). Although some Aztalan radiocarbon dates may suggest a very long occupation, a reappraisal suggests that the more reasonable range of dates is from
about A.D. 1100 to 1300 (Baerreis and Bryson 1965: 209). These authors also
discuss midwestern climate changes in relation to Mississippian expansion defining
the Neo-Atlantic episode as a period from about A.D. 800 to 1250 which had
mild winters and generally favorable agricultural conditions. This was followed
by the Pacific episode, A.D. 1250-1450, when the climate became much less
favorable for agriculture in some regions. During this period the catastrophic
reduction of the Anasazi territory occurred in the southwest, and Upper Re-
publican corn farming ceased on the plains, either the people or their culture
shifting southward into Oklahoma. "The plains economy extended eastward
with an apparent expansion of the prairie peninsula (Bryson and Baerreis 1964)
perhaps 'amputating' the northern outposts of the Middle Mississippi peoples
in Wisconsin and Minnesota" (Baerreis and Bryson 1965: 216). For about a
century, A.D. 1450 to 1550, the climate reverted back to the more favorable
conditions characteristic of Neo-Atlantic times, but it was followed by more

unfavorable growing conditions, termed the Neo-Boreal, or descriptively, as the "Little Ice Age." The Neo-Boreal lasted from 1550 to 1880 ending with the recent climatic amelioration. "Unfortunately for the North American cultural historian, the Neo-Boreal began just at the time of European contact, obscuring the relative roles of cultural and climatic impact on the lifeways of the Indian. It is an intriguing possibility that deteriorating climatic conditions making an agricultural economy precarious may have been more influential in producing a shift to a fur trading economy than the magnet of European trade goods." (*Ibid.* 217). Within this climate sequence they suggest that expansion of Mississippian influences occurred *during and not after* the favorable Neo-Atlantic episode, and accept the Carcajou Point dates indicating that the Oneota ceramic tradition was already in existence by A.D. 1000.

No longhouse structures have been reported from Wisconsin Oneota sites; either they do not occur, or their size and unexpected form has escaped notice in small excavations. A clue suggesting their possible appearance may be present. Outside the stockade at Aztalan excavations outlined a very large house, 28 by 40 feet, with central supports suggesting the ridge and gable roof construction. No daub is reported, and the absence of double post holes suggests mat rather than bark sheathing. The excavators (Wittry and Baerreis 1958: 64-67) identified the structure as a summer lodge. A wall trench appears along part of the two sides, three corners have doorways, and the length does not approach the size of many longhouses; features which differ from the Grant site. On the other hand Pike reported Osage longhouses varied from 30 to 100 feet, and so the width may be diagnostic rather than length. The sides are not exactly parallel, but both ends suggest a sub-rounded shape, rather than the rectangular Middle Mississippian form. The corner doorways are possibly reminiscent of a similar placement in some southeastern ceremonial structures summarized in Howard (1968: 134, 136).

The Midway site near La Crosse in southwestern Wisconsin was originally considered part of the Ioway-Orr Oneota grouping (Griffin 1937: 181, McKern 1945), but when Orr pottery from the nearby Upper Iowa valley was fully described Mildred Wedel (1959: 121) concluded "If Midway is retained in the Orr Focus then it must be recognized that its relationship to the other sites is different from their apparent relationship to each other." It was termed an "aberrant Orr Focus site" by Hall (1962, vol. 1: 12) and was restudied in a 1965 master's thesis by Gibbon which I have not yet read. Henning (1970: 149-150) after briefly reviewing the literature, groups it within his Orr Phase, but notes the problems. The original site report by McKern (1945) contains no discussion of house structures.

The Bell site is identified as an historic Fox settlement in Wisconsin occupied after this group left their territory east of Lake Michigan during the Iroquois Wars. The village had a stockade ditch, and the only complete house, excavated during preliminary exploration, was a rectangular lodge 16 by 30 feet, largely outlined by a wall trench. Systematic excavations found a circular wigwam and sections of wall trench and post mold alignments (Wittry 1963). The example is of interest because this Algonquin speaking group was intrusive into the Mississippi drainage during the eighteenth century, and their houses and fortification wall at the Bell site do not fit the Oneota pattern, nor would one expect them to at this time.

IOWA The absence of Oneota house structures in the 1930s excavations along the Upper Iowa River was interpreted by Mildred Wedel as an indication that the evidence had been destroyed by plowing.

> No evidence of Indian houses was found by Dr. Keyes and Mr. Orr on the village terraces. This suggests that they were rectangular or elliptical structures built with a pole framework and covered with bark slabs or reed matting, and with a central fireplace, like the dwellings used by Indians living in the woodland areas to the east. Frequent plowing would soon have destroyed the only certain vestiges of their existence—the fireplaces and post-holes. Many pits dug into the ground to serve as small storage cellars were found; in fact, more than fifty were dug out at the Lane Enclosure site. Some may have been within houses, serving as closets do nowadays for stowing away personal possessions and provisions, but most were probably outside and used only for food storage. (Mildred Wedel 1961: 584-585).

Two illustrations of Ioway oval bark lodges from Kansas accompany the article. The cover to the article shows an inaccurate artist's reconstruction of an Indian village with round, bark-over-mat lodges and a birch bark canoe, an illustration not chosen by the author. It seems probable that Middle Mississippian rectangular structures with wall trenches would have been observed by Keyes and Orr, despite their lack of professional training and experience in defining structures. Post rows were regularly missed in their excavations until Orr later began clearing Glenwood-Nebraska earth lodges in southwest Iowa. Post molds at the Grant site and probably others along the Upper Iowa do seem to penetrate well into subsoil, undisturbed by surface plowing. I think Mildred Wedel was correct in assuming that small lodges with a single fireplace were in use. A reappraisal suggests the evidence of structures should still be present at most Oneota sites along the Upper Iowa, and some should be longhouses with deep substantial posts.

Excavations at the Kingston site (Straffin 1971) in southeast Iowa identified no house posts around the storage pits, but the area cleared was very small. In the central Des Moines Valley, Gradwohl (1965) has named the Moingoina Phase, represented by a distinctive Goodhue Oneota pottery which is different from either Correctionville-Blue Earth or Orr. No wall trenches were present, but a very long line of substantial posts was found. He is hesitant to definitely assign a structural function to the line, since it could be a stockade, house, or associated with the mortuary complex (personal communication 1970). It separated the village area from the burials. Smithsonian dates for the Goodhue and Mohler Farm sites cited by Henning are respectively 1650 ± 200 and 1500 ±

200, 1680 ± 180.

The McKinney site has an octagonal enclosure, and in this context it is interesting to note Norris reported the Lane Enclosure to be somewhat irregularly polygonal. The McKinney site has been tentatively assigned to the Orr Phase by Henning (1970: 149) but Straffin (1971: 3) reports that the small surface collection of pottery does not seem typical. The site probably contains more than one component. A small test excavation by Richard Slattery and George Horton in 1970 may clarify the relationships. No house structures were found. I have looked at rim sherds in The University of Iowa Archaeological Laboratory (accession 48) and those obtained from the 1970 investigation. The pottery is distinct from that of the Lane Enclosure.

ILLINOIS   Excavations by Bluhm *et al.* (1961) south of Chicago found oval ended houses, some of them having considerable length, and the structures have been summarized in table 3 and are discussed further in Chapter 5. These are not longhouses by the definition of width, for they are only 13 feet wide, too small for pairs of families living across from each other. The length of some houses, together with the central posts and ridge construction suggests they may be an analogous or a derived form from larger houses. Ceramic resemblances with Orr Focus Oneota were recognized in the original reports. These two sites were assigned to Blue Island culture by Quimby (1960: 105) who noted the culture "was similar to the Lake Winnebago culture and probably represents an ancient occupancy of the Chicago area by one of the Chiwere Siouan groups, perhaps an offshoot of the ancestral Iowa, Oto, or Missouri in the period from about A.D. 1300 to 1600." More recently Henning (1970: 150-151) assigned both sites to the Orr Phase in Illinois. A comparison of the rim profiles shows forms which do not occur in the Upper Iowa examples. Comparing our figure 43 A to N shows almost all thinned or rounded rim lips. Other forms such as extruded, beveled, and thickened occur in the following frequencies: Lane Enclosure est. 2%, Grant site 0%, Anker site 44%, Oak Forest 30%. The Anker and Oak Forest rim types lumped together in the comparison are designated A, E, G, G-I, H, and L (Bluhm *et al.* 1961, figures 56 and 73). Assuming that the Illinois designated type E parallels Iowa forms reduces the totals: Anker 25%, and Oak Forest 19%. The decoration trait frequencies also differ considerably. The inclusion of these two Illinois sites within the Orr Phase should be reexamined, and I tend to favor Quimby's solution over Henning's.

MISSOURI   The Missouri Chiwere Siouan group have been identified as occupying the Utz site in historic times estimated at prior to 1673 until as late as 1728 (Bray 1963: 2). Utz site structures identified from post molds were "in an elliptical pattern and enclosing fire hearths and large bell-shaped storage pits. The Missouri Indian houses were of the general wigwam or long-house shape, similar to those of the Iowa, built of a framework of poles and covered with woven mats" (Chapman 1964: 93). At the Gumbo Point townsite "part of a pattern of post molds was excavated which makes it appear that at least one type of house used by the Missouri was rectangular and rather long, similar to the 'long houses' used by some Eastern tribes" (Bray 1961a: 222). The report on Gumbo Point site describes this house in detail. It is very small, 9 to 10 feet wide and more than 25 feet long, has center support posts, and with one slightly rounded end (Chapman 1959: 41-46). Called a "long house" it is actually more typical of the small lodges. The single rather than double post holes suggest mat sheathing. An unidentified structure appears to be represented by a much longer post row adjacent to this house (*Ibid.* see his figure 33).

The Osage archaeological house evidence shows a "rectangular ground plan with multiple center posts, straight-sided, teardrop-shaped, and bell-shaped pits for storage within the houses, and rectangular trench refuse pits. Small pits approximately a foot in diameter and filled with charred corncobs or wood may have been used for smoking skins. These smoke pits were also within the house structures. Excavations have revealed houses thirty-one to forty-two feet long and fifteen to twenty-two feet wide" (Chapman 1964:96). The two investigations at the Little Osage village site found the house evidence destroyed by cultivation, although a few posts found indicated the presence of a pole frame construction (Chapman 1959: 11). The Osage have Oneota-like pottery and may possibly be derived from the Neosho Focus in the four corner area of Missouri, Kansas, Oklahoma, and Arkansas (Chapman 1964: 94). I am not familiar in detail with the complex archaeological patterns in Missouri, but the review of the preceding sources shows the Missouri had narrow, relatively long houses, not comparable with the Grant site; larger houses seem to be present among the Osage.

ARKANSAS   A recent non-technical summary shows an artist's reconstruction of the Quapaw bark-covered longhouse with curved roof, rectangular ends, end entryways, and lacking an exterior framework. The Osage of Missouri used northern Arkansas primarily as a hunting territory, and none of their village or camp sites have been identified (McGimsey 1969: 36-41). Some problems emerge in the archaeological evidence. The Menard site is identified as the Quapaw village of Osotouy on the Arkansas River by James A. Ford who summarizes previous excavations and describes his own in detail. He found incomplete post rows and one complete structure.

> Rather ragged lines of post moulds outline a rectangular building that measures about 30 feet east to west and 20 feet north to south. At least one partition can be traced across the eastern end of the structure. This building has two superimposed floors that demonstrate how these low house mounds were accumulated. The lower floor formed of packed clay is littered with refuse. However, black midden soil, ash, bones, and broken pottery evidently accumulated more rapidly about the walls of the building than inside on the floor. The floor was probably swept occasionally and the refuse thrown

immediately outside the house. Consequently, the house floor became a depression in relation to the surrounding ground surface, and it must have been difficult to keep out rain water and maintain a dry floor. The Indians corrected this situation by bringing in clean yellow clay and covering the old floor to a depth of 10 inches. Additional refuse and three well-burned fireplaces rested on this new surface. One fireplace was at the west end of the building, one in the center towards the west end, and one about the middle of the length of the structure near the south wall (Ford 1961: 152).

The house plan (Ford 1961: 154) lacks wall trenches. Double post groups along the north wall possibly suggest bark sheathing, and a few occur along the south and end walls. The interior east end has well-defined interior post series which may be the end platform, straight along the interior edge, irregular in shape against the outer wall. This feature varies in width from just under 4 to 6 feet wide. The settlement pattern with temple and house mounds, and the complex lower Mississippian pottery types bear no resemblance to Oneota. A 1968 personal communication by Preston Holder to Henning (1970: 147) states the opinion that the main Quapaw seventeenth and eighteenth century settlement was the nearby Dupree site, not Menard, a problem for others to resolve.

PLAINS ONEOTA   Oneota sites are rare west of the Missouri River, none occurring more than fifty miles from the main stream; and this culture is regarded as a prairie rather than a plains entity (Waldo Wedel 1961: 117). Contact with plains cultures sometimes influenced house construction, illustrated by the Leary site House 1, a semi-subterranean earth lodge. In plan it was 20 by 21 feet across, square shaped with rounded corners, with the 15 foot entryway passage to the west. It contained a central fireplace, and 4 roof supports. Both internal and external storage pits occurred as well as burials. Only two inside pits were definitely being associated with the house, and stratigraphic evidence showed the house was later than some of the other village remains and the burial beneath it. Systematic excavations for house structures failed to find additional examples leading the excavators to suggest that "the typical structure may have been of a more perishable nature, possibly a bark covered lodge on a framework of poles, erected on or only a few inches below the ground surface, and subsequently destroyed by the plow" (Hill and Wedel 1936: 19, see 15-19). In Kansas the earth lodge form occurs at the prehistoric Fanning site, identified with reservations as associated with the Kansa tribe; and this house form is also present at two historic Kansa villages, Doniphan and Blue River (Waldo Wedel 1959: 171, 128, 190). There are no reports of longhouses at the relatively few plains Oneota archaeological sites west of the Missouri. A survey of possible pottery relationships appears in Henning (1970: 142-152). The Redbird Focus of northeastern Nebraska is tentatively assigned to the Ponca and the pottery is not within the Oneota Tradition, although some Orr Focus trade pottery appears. The report by Wood (1965) indicates earth lodges were the major house form.

THE GRANT POTTERY TYPE   When I first read Henning's excellent 1970 study of Oneota pottery relationships and his identification of phases, it initially appeared that he was simply following the trend of obliterating the long established usage of the Midwestern Taxonomic Method. Renaming the Orr Focus the Orr Phase seemed no more than a reversal of the Biblical caution, putting old wine into new bottles, giving a long recognized taxonomic entity a variation in name. In working with the study it soon became apparent that very different relationships and definitions were being applied in practice. A potentially diverse group of components are now grouped within the Orr Phase, ranging geographically from Blue Island culture occupying the eastern Lake Michigan frontier of the Oneota Tradition near Indiana; through parts of Wisconsin, Minnesota, Iowa, Missouri, beyond the Mississippi Valley and its western tributaries; through the Missouri Valley westward into Kansas and Nebraska. To this distribution we may add southeastern South Dakota, the Oneota Ioway site identified by Mildred Wedel (Mott 1938: 302). Chronologically many of these various components are relatively late, after A.D. 1300, but others are early and may span five to seven centuries with the anticipation of adding a century more with further radiocarbon dating. The pottery included within the proposed Orr Phase has repeatedly been differentiated as aberrant, different, similar, or resembling the Allamakee Trailed type from the Upper Iowa in the original reports where it is described, but seldom is it identical without substantial qualifications. Given this definition of the Orr Phase the Grant pottery type does not exist. It is just a minor variant, more similar to Allamakee Trailed than some other varieties in the phase.

This comment is not intended to detract from an obviously important restudy of the enigmatic Oneota. Yet a very major taxonomic problem sooner or later must be reckoned with: by-passing the disadvantages of the Midwestern Taxonomic Method has lost its advantages. The system had strength in allowing for intermediate degrees of relationships, some agreement over dimensional similarity and description, and a stability in definition that lasted for three decades of research. One of the weaknesses of the Method was chronology and temporal succession. Yet this same problem is reappearing in a different form, for if we add the Grant site to the Orr Phase there is an undifferentiated seven centuries, and we may anticipate similar problems in many areas of Orr Phase occurrence.

I think that Henning is correct in showing relationships among a potentially very large number of components, but the inevitable question arises, do they show a common phase relationship? What are intervening degrees of relationship between the Orr Phase and its components? The use of the concept *group continuity* as connecting links raises problems in dealing with mobile groups over centuries of time and one cannot but feel nostalgia for less connotative terminology used in previous years. Alternatives are available to the Orr Phase as currently perceived. One might call the Orr Phase grouping a ceramic series, a macro-phase, or a sub-tradition, leaving room for such smaller entities as the Orr Focus as previously defined.

The Grant type is a ceramic unit which will be accepted or ignored through usage and its viability cannot yet be predicted. It will, I think, prove useful to differentiate this early assemblage of decoration traits from those appearing elsewhere, temporally and spatially, and to this degree the taxonomy should reflect the differences, but the term type is at best a compromise, a reflection of cultural relationships interpreted from pottery description. It is my impression that with Grant pottery defined relatively to later Lane Enclosure samples, it will now make it possible to isolate further components of the Grant type and arrive at an expanded definition of Grant pottery. If this proves possible the compromise terminology will have served its purpose.

SUMMARY For purposes of the discussion by other archaeologists which follows this report, the main conclusions from the Grant village study may be summarized as follows:

(1) *The Griffin hypothesis has been shown to be inapplicable in a major area of Oneota occurrence.* The 1960 prediction that early Oneota Aspect houses would be Middle Mississippian in form was a logical assumption and may well apply in areas where the transition to Oneota actually took place. It has limited application at Carcajou Point, but not in the Upper Iowa Valley where Oneota appears very early. The survey of Oneota excavations indicates common use of pole frame construction for a variety of house types but a general absence of wattle and daub house wall construction.

(2) *The longhouse type can be confirmed as present at the time of European exploration in many areas of the Mississippi drainage.* The review of historic and ethnographic sources shows that a variety of longhouse forms were in common use among a number of Siouan speaking tribes, apparently as residential units for lineages or clans. The archaeological evidence of longhouses is incomplete, contradictory, or lacking from most areas, but the identification of this structural type from post molds at the Grant site gains considerable plausibility when the widespread distribution is recognized from the historic narratives.

(3) *The longhouse abandonment can be documented among various tribes.* The late nineteenth and twentieth century studies of midwestern tribes did not generally point out the significance of the lineage or clan residential houses because they had long since fallen into disuse. The survey of the literature gives tantalizing, if incomplete, fragments of the decline of this house type. Although survivals in form occur, most tribes had abandoned these large houses by the 1820s, and they may well have been falling into disuse among some tribes a century earlier.

(4) *An explanation for the abandonment of this house type can be made.* The Iroquois of central New York shifted from longhouses to individual or ex-

tended family dwellings late in the eighteenth century, a reflection of changes in social, economic, and political conditions brought about by increased European contact and control of the area. This represents a seemingly parallel case with the Mississippi River groups, who completed the shift to smaller lodges some decades after the Iroquois, as the frontier along the Mississippi was more fully opened to the fur trade. The breakdown of traditional values seems to have been accompanied by growing individualism and extended family emphasis, with a consequent decline of clan and lineage kin allegiance. Under the impact of social and economic changes resulting from increased European interaction, the larger residential kin groups apparently became less important, dooming the longhouse as a cultural alternative among the Siouan speaking tribes remaining in the Mississippi drainage sometime previous to the shift from American trade to occupation by American settlers.

(5) *The origin of longhouses remains an unresolved question.* Because the term longhouse is so intimately connected with the Iroquois, Griffin has suggested to me that it would be more suitable to give a different name to the midwestern examples. The type seems to parallel the New York examples, and so the name is retained as a descriptive term with no implications of a common origin. The term itself is variously spelled as two words or one, and I have followed Ritchie's usage (1965). The apparently early appearance of longhouses in the upper midwest, and the occurrence of this type at least intermittently as far south as the Quapaw of Arkansas raises a question about origins and remotely possible connections with similar structures occurring in the northeast and southeast United States. Despite variations, the longhouses in eastern North America conceivably could have had a common origin, being more readily acquired by tribes with a nascent clan residential system. Such a hypothetical reconstruction must be held in abeyance, for numerous archaeological problems remain in every local sequence, and the multi-family residence may be neither early nor even present in most areas.

(6) *A summer residential pattern appears related to longhouse usage in the Mississippi Valley.* Unfortunately the Grant site faunal analysis does not provide evidence of seasonality or lack of it. Our evaluation of birds previously identified from the Anker and Oak Knoll sites suggests these smaller Oneota houses were occupied during the summer months. The explorers found longhouses in use during their summer visits, and several describe the shift into smaller houses during the winter, a pattern contrasting with the Iroquois year round use.

(7) *A village population was calculated.* Population estimates are lacking from other Oneota sites. The village perimeter was outlined on two sides by the terrace edge, and at other points was determined by the absence of storage pits, and occupational debris in the trenches. Defined in this way the village area barely exceeded an acre in size, with houses grouped around a central open area. Assuming a floor plan providing space for ten families, or fifty people, and an average of four lodges simultaneously occupied, the village size was 200 inhabi-

tants. The projection is based on a number of assumptions about variables, and the structure usage did change over the years. While the total might be halved, I think it unlikely to be doubled. This village size is comparable in area to Oak Forest and the Lane Enclosure Oneota sites, and is about equal to the nearby Hartley Fort Woodland encampment on the terrace. These well-defined village areas contrast markedly with reports of huge Oneota sites on the terraces of the Upper Iowa, and elsewhere in this state and in the midwest. There undoubtedly were much larger villages than the Grant site, but the larger or largest sites may prove to successive, adjacent occupations, not yet recognized in current Oneota ceramic classifications.

(8) *The Grant type is proposed as an Oneota archaeological manifestation.* Grant ceramics as a group are separable from the Lane Enclosure and other late Oneota sites in the Upper Iowa Valley having Allamakee Trailed pottery. The main distinquishing traits on Grant pottery are a greater use of medium lines, lack of punctate filled design areas, lack of narrow rim notches, rarity of the wedge form, and an emphasis on medium and wide notches. The Grant pottery seems to be related to the late Allamakee Trailed, the rim profiles being comparable, and some other traits being similar. The conspicuous differences in leached shell temper are either the result of age or soil differences in the sites. So far the Grant site is unique, but I anticipate other components of the phase will be identified in the area. The Grant type and Allamakee Trailed type may eventually be linked together into a *group continuity* with an intermediate development being presently missing or unidentified, but the Grant ceramic description should now make it possible to restudy the problem. Very distinctive differences set off the Upper Iowa Oneota pottery from that found in the Kingston-Chariton River series and from the Correctionville-Blue Earth series. The definition of the Grant type and its chronological position appears to negate the proposed Correctionville-Blue Earth series ancestry of the Allamakee Trailed type of Orr Phase ceramics, a theory first proposed by Wilford and held in abeyance by Henning (1970: 154), since no known or obvious convergences appear as the two series progress backwards in time.

(9) *The early dates and cultural succession on the terrace appear to answer a question raised about "pre-Oneota" Mississippian antecedents in this region.* The abandonment of the Late Woodland Hartley Fort in the early tenth century was closely followed by the eleventh century Grant people, leaving no clear or prolonged opening for a Middle Mississippian settlement on the terrace. The ancestor of Orr Oneota seems to be earlier, but fully developed Oneota. The transition or development from Middle Mississippian culture did not occur in the Upper Iowa Valley, the area where Oneota culture was first archaeologically defined in the midwest, and which was originally believed to be a developmental center. Thus, there are many loose ends which require resolution, and we may well anticipate controversies over the preceding interpretations and conclusions drawn from the investigations, which nevertheless offer new directions in Oneota

research, and emphasizes the significance of regional variation in North American prehistoric cultural development.

8. APPENDIX: FAUNAL IDENTIFICATION BY HOLMES A. SEMKEN

Examination of vertebrate remains from the Grant site revealed the presence of at least fourteen taxa: three fish, two turtles, one snake, one bird, and seven mammals. The fauna, which is cataloged into the Department of Geology collections, is too small for statistical comparisons but adequate for generalized environmental conclusions. Sorting by archaeological provenience did not reveal a distribution pattern so the remains are treated as a single local fauna. Geology catalogue numbers are applied to each taxon. Individual elements also bear archaeological provenience numbers.

TELEOSTOMI
Aplodinotus grunniens (freshwater drum), 34762, 5 individuals: 5 pharyngeal bars.

Ictalurus punctatus (channel catfish), 34763, 2 individuals: 3 pectoral spines, 3 opercula, 2 hyomandibulae, 1 maxillary, and 1 dentary. The larger individual was collected from cache pit 13.

Ictiobus niger (black buffalo fish), 39561, 1 individual: suboperculum.

REPTILIA
Trionyx spinifer (softshell turtle), 34764, 1 individual: complete carapace less vertebrals.

Emydin turtle (not identified), 34765, 2 individuals: 4 plastron and carapace fragments.

Snake (not identified), 34766, one vertebra.

AVES
Bird (not identified), 34768, ulna, distal portion; femur, proximal portion; carpometacarpus fragment; tarsometatarsus, proximal portion; clavicle fragment.

MAMMALIA
Blarina brevicauda (shorttail shrew), 34772, 1 individual: upper incisor, left mandible, right mandible in same stage of wear. From cache pit 7B.

Castor canadensis (beaver), 34769, 1 individual: RM^1.

Synaptomys cooperi (southern bog lemming), 34771, 1 individual: LM_1.

Peromyscus sp. (deer mouse), 34770, 1 individual: left mandible with M_{1-3}. From cache pit 13.

Cervus canadensis (wapiti), 34775, 1 individual: RM_3, antler fragment, 12 phalange fragments, 1 astragalus, proximal scapula fragment.

Odocoileus virginianus (whitetail deer), 34773, 4 individuals: 4 lower rt. mandibles, one with M_3, one with P_4-M_3, one with M_2-$_3$, and one with P_4-M_3; RP_2; RP_3; 2 cervical vertebrae, rt. astragalus; rt. calcaneus;

1f. calcaneus; 4 terminal phalanges; distal portion tibia, 2 sesamoids;
2 proximal phalanges; distal portion metapodial; and 2 antler tips.
Canis familiaris (domestic dog), 34774, 3 individuals; right mandible
with complete dentition; right mandible with M_2; RM_1 (too large to belong
to the previous specimen); RM_2; RP_2; LM^1 fragment; axis, tibia, 2 scapulae.

COMMENTS   All taxa identified presently reside in Iowa or were common in
the eastern part of the state until the 1850s (John Bowles, personal communication). In addition, the distribution of the above taxa in all surrounding states
precludes observation of a minor climatic change on range fluctuations during
the occupation period. The catfish, drum, black buffalo fish, softshell turtle,
and beaver demonstrate the proximity of a substantial body of water. Forests,
suggested by the relative abundance of deer and the beaver, interspersed by
marshy areas (bog lemming) were in the immediate vicinity of the site.

It may be significant that the whitetail deer is known from four right and
no left mandibles. While the sample is small and this distribution may be due
to chance, Cleland (1966: 217-220) noted a marked predominance of right
mandibles from the Moccasin Bluff site refuse pits and suggested that left mandibles were saved for a purpose. Each mandible was recovered from a different
feature: cache pits 14, 23, 35, 40 and square B24. It should be noted that the
three domestic dog jaws are rights as well. Dental wear stage ages proposed by
Severinghaus (1949) and illustrated by Cockrum (1962) indicate that all deer
were killed between 4½ and 7 years of age.

9. REFERENCES

Anderson, Adrian A.
   1971   Review of Iowa River Valley Archaeology. *Prehistoric Investigations.*
           report 3, no. 1. State Archaeologist, The University of Iowa Pub-
           lications, Iowa City.

Baerreis, David A. and Reid A. Bryson
   1965   Climatic Episodes and the Dating of the Mississippian Cultures.
           The Wisconsin Archeologist, vol. 46, no. 4: 203-220. Milwaukee.

   1967   Climatic Change and the Mill Creek Culture of Iowa. *Archives of
           Archaeology,* no. 29. Society for American Archaeology, Univer-
           sity of Wisconsin Press. (Part I reprinted in *Iowa Archaeological
           Society Journal,* vol. 15, 1968: 1-191. Part II in press, Westfield.)

Barrett, S.A.
   1933   Ancient Aztalan. *Milwaukee Public Museum Bulletin,* vol. 13,
           Milwaukee.

Bluhm, Elaine A. and Gloria Fenner
   1961   The Oak Forest Site. Chicago Area Archaeology. *Illinois Archae-
           ological Survey Bulletin* 3: 138-161, Urbana.

Bluhm, Elaine A. and Allen Liss
   1961   The Anker Site. Chicago Area Archaeology. *Illinois Archaeological
           Survey Bulletin* 3: 89-137, Urbana.

Bray, Robert T.
   1961   The Flynn Cemetery: An Orr Focus Burial Site in Allamakee
           County. *Iowa Archaeological Society Journal,* vol. 10, no. 4:
           15-25, Iowa City.

   1961a   The Missouri Indian Tribe in Archaeology and History. *Missouri
           Historical Review,* vol. 55, no. 3: 213-225, Columbia.

   1963   Southern Cult Motifs from the Utz Oneota Site, Saline County,
           Missouri. *Missouri Archaeologist,* vol. 25: 1-40, Columbia.

Bushnell, David I.
   1922   Villages of the Algonquian, Siouan and Caddoan Tribes West of
           the Mississippi. *Bureau of American Ethnology Bulletin* 77,
           Washington, D.C.

Catlin, George
1841   *Letters and Notes on the Manners, Customs, and Conditions of the North American Indians.* vol. 1, New York.

Chapman, Carl H.
1959   The Little Osage and Missouri Indian Village Sites ca. 1727-77 A.D. *Missouri Archaeologist*, vol. 21, no. 1: 1-69, Columbia.

Chapman, Carl H. and Eleanor F. Chapman
1964   *Indians and Archaeology of Missouri.* Missouri Handbook no. 6, University of Missouri Press, Columbia.

Cleland, Charles E.
1966   The Prehistoric Animal Ecology and Ethnozoology of the Upper Great Lakes Region. *Anthropological Papers, Museum of Anthropology,* no. 29. University of Michigan, Ann Arbor.

Cockrum, E.L.
1962   *Introduction to Mammalogy.* Ronald Press, New York.

Cooke, W.W.
1888   Report on Bird Migration in the Mississippi Valley in the Years 1884 and 1885. *U.S. Department of Agriculture,* 7365 Bulletin no. 2. Government Printing Office, Washington, D.C.

Driver, Harold E.
1969   *Indians of North America.* The University of Chicago Press, Chicago. (second edition)

Driver, Harold E. and William C. Massey
1957   Comparative Studies of North American Indians. *Transactions of the American Philosophical Society,* vol. 47: 165-456. Philadelphia.

Fletcher, Alice C. and Francis la Flesche
1911   The Omaha Tribe. *Bureau of American Ethnology Annual Report* 27, Washington, D.C.

Ford, James A.
1961   Menard Site: The Quapaw Village of Osotouy on the Arkansas River. *Anthropological Papers, American Museum of Natural History,* vol. 48, part 2: 133-191, New York.

Gibbon, Guy
    1970   A Brief History of Oneota Research in Wisconsin. *Wisconsin Magazine of History*, vol. 53, no. 4: 278-293, Madison.

Gradwohl, David M.
    1965   Archaeological Investigations in the Red Rock Reservoir, Iowa, 1964. *Plains Anthropologist*, vol. 10, no. 27: 49-50, Lincoln.

Griffin, James B.
    1937   The Archaeological Remains of the Chiwere Sioux. *American Antiquity*, vol. 2: 180-181, Menasha.

    1960   A Hypothesis for the Prehistory of the Winnebago (pp. 809-865). *Culture in History*, Stanley Diamond, ed. Brandeis University, New York.

    1961   Some Correlations of Climatic and Cultural Change in Eastern North American Prehistory. *Annals, New York Academy of Sciences*, vol. 95, art. 1: 710-717, New York.

    1964   The Northeast Woodlands Area (pp. 223-258). *Prehistoric Man in the New World*, Jesse D. Jennings and Edward Norbeck, eds. The University of Chicago Press, Chicago.

    1967   Eastern North American Archaeology: A Summary. *Science*, vol. 156, no. 3772: 175-191, Washington, D.C.

Hall, Robert L.
    1962   *The Archeology of Carcajou Point*. 2 vols. University of Wisconsin Press, Madison.

    1966MS Cahokia Chronology. Paper prepared for the Annual Meeting of the Central States Anthropological Society in St. Louis, Missouri, April 28-30, 1966, St. Louis.

    1967   The Mississippian Heartland and Its Plains Relationship. *Plains Anthropologist*, vol. 12, no. 36: 175-183, Lincoln.

Henning, Dale R.
    1961   Oneota Ceramics in Iowa. *Iowa Archaeological Society Journal*, vol. 11, no. 2: 1-47 ff, Iowa City.

    1967   Mississippian Influences on the Eastern Plains Border: An Evaluation. *Plains Anthropologist*, vol. 12, no. 36: 184-194, Lincoln.

    1970   Development and Interrelationships of Oneota Culture in the lower Missouri River Valley. *Missouri Archaeologist*, vol. 32: 1-180, Columbia.

Henning, Dale R. and Martin Q. Peterson
　1965　Re-articulated Burials from the Upper Iowa River Valley. *Iowa Archaeological Society Journal*, vol. 13: 1-16, McGregor.

Hill, A.T. and Waldo R. Wedel
　1936　Excavations at the Leary Indian Village and Burial Site, Richardson County, Nebraska. *Nebraska History Magazine*, vol. 17, no. 1: 2-73, Lincoln.

Howard, James H.
　1965　The Ponca Tribe. *Bureau of American Ethnology Bulletin* 195, Washington, D.C.

　1968　The Southeastern Ceremonial Complex and Its Interpretation. *Missouri Archaeological Society Memoir*, no. 6: 1-169, Columbia.

Jackson, Donald (ed.)
　1966　*The Journals of Zebulon Montgomery Pike: with Letters and Related Documents.* 2 vols. University of Oklahoma Press, Norman.

Jenkins, John T. and Holmes A. Semken
　1971MS Faunal Analysis of the Lane Enclosure, Allamakee County, Iowa. *Iowa Academy of Science Proceedings,* vol. 78, no. 3-4: 76-78.

Jennings, Jesse D.
　1968　*Prehistory of North America.* McGraw-Hill, New York.

Keyes, Charles R.
　1927　Prehistoric Man in Iowa. *The Palimpsest,* vol. 8, no. 6: 185-230. State Historical Society, Iowa City.

　1951　Prehistoric Indians of Iowa. *The Palimpsest,* vol. 32, no. 8: 285-342. State Historical Society, Iowa City.

Kinietz, William Vernon
　1965　*The Indians of the Western Great Lakes.* University of Michigan Press, Ann Arbor.

Logan, Wilfred
　1959MS Analysis of Woodland Complexes in Northeastern Iowa. Ph.D. Thesis, Department of Anthropology, University of Michigan (Microfilm), Ann Arbor.

McGee, W.J.
    1897   The Siouan Indians: A Preliminary Sketch. *Bureau of American Ethnology Annual Report* 15: 157-204, Washington, D.C.

McKern, W.C.
    1939   The Midwestern Taxonomic Method as an Aid to Archaeological Study. *American Antiquity,* vol. 4, no. 4: 301-313. Menasha.

    1945   Preliminary Report of the Upper Mississippi Phase in Wisconsin. *Milwaukee Public Museum Bulletin,* vol. 16, no. 3: 109-285. Milwaukee.

McKusick, Marshall B.
    1963   Evaluation and Index, Iowa Archaeological Reports. (see Ellison Orr).

    1964   *Men of Ancient Iowa.* Iowa State University Press, Ames.

    1964a   Prehistoric Man in Northeastern Iowa. *The Palimpsest,* vol. 45, no. 12: 465-494. State Historical Society, Iowa City.

    1971   Oneota Longhouses. *Prehistoric Investigations,* report 3, no. 6, State Archaeologist, The University of Iowa Publications, Iowa City.

    1971a   Art That Predates Columbus. *The Iowan,* vol. 19, no. 4: 8-13 ff. Shenandoah.

    1971b   Reminiscences of a Pioneer Boy by Ellison Orr, with a foreword by Marshall McKusick. *Annals of Iowa,* vol. 40, nos. 7 & 8, pp. 530-560, 593-630. State Department of History, Des Moines.

Morgan, Lewis Henry
    1954   *League of the Ho-de-no-sau-nee or Iroquois.* Human Relations Area Files Reprint. 2 vols. New Haven. (Lloyd edition of 1901. The 1851 first edition is not annotated).

Mott, Mildred
    1938   The Relation of Historic Indian Tribes to Archaeological Manifestations in Iowa. *Iowa Journal of History and Politics,* vol. 36, no. 3: 227-314.

Orr, Ellison
    1914   Indian Pottery of the Oneota or Upper Iowa River Valley in Northeastern Iowa. *Iowa Academy of Science Proceedings,* vol. 21: 231-239.

    1949MS The Rock Shelters of the Oneota Dolomite in Allamakee County, Iowa. Manuscript, Effigy Mounds National Monument. Copy University of Iowa Archaeological Laboratory, Iowa City.

1963   Iowa Archaeological Reports 1934-1939 With an Evaluation and Index by Marshall McKusick. *Archives of Archaeology,* no. 20. Society for American Archaeology, University of Wisconsin Press, Madison.

Peske, G. Richard
1966   Oneota Settlement Patterns and Agricultural Patterns in Winnebago County. *Wisconsin Archaeologist,* vol. 47, no. 4: 188-195, Milwaukee.

Plank, Pryor
1908   The Iowa, Sac and Fox Indian Mission and Its Missionaries, Rev. Samuel M. Irvin and Wife. *Kansas State Historical Society, Transactions,* vol. 10, pp. 312-325, Topeka.

Quimby, George I.
1960   *Indian Life in the Upper Great Lakes: 11,000 B.C. to A.D. 1800.* University of Chicago Press, Chicago.

Radin, Paul
1923   The Winnebago Tribe. *Bureau of American Ethnology, Annual Report* 37, Washington, D.C.

Ritchie, William
1965   *The Archaeology of New York State.* Natural History Press, Garden City, New York.

Schoolcraft, Henry
1857   *Information Respecting the History, Condition and Prospects of the Indian Tribes of the United States.* vol. 4. Lippincott, Grambo and Co., Philadelphia.

Severinghaus, C.W.
1949   Tooth Development and Wear as Criteria of Age in White-Tailed Deer. *Journal of Wildlife Management,* 13: 195-216, Washington, D.C.

Skinner, Alanson
1926   Ethnology of the Ioway Indians. *Milwaukee Public Museum Bulletin,* vol. 5, no. 4: 181-354, Milwaukee.

1926a   The Mascoutens or Prairie Potawatomi Indians. Part 2: Notes on Material Culture. *Milwaukee Public Museum Bulletin,* vol. 6, no. 2: 263-326, Milwaukee.

Starr, Frederick
    1897   Bibliography and Summary of the Archaeology of Iowa. *Davenport Academy of Natural Sciences Proceedings,* vol. 6: 7-24, 53-124, Davenport.
    1897a   Circular of Suggestions Regarding Work in Archaeology. *Davenport Academy of Natural Sciences Proceedings,* vol. 6: 340-343, Davenport.

Straffin, Dean
    1971   *The Kingston Oneota Site.* State Archaeologist, report 2, The University of Iowa Publications, Iowa City.

Struever, Stuart
    1968   Woodland Subsistence-Settlement Systems in the Lower Illinois Valley (pp. 285-313). *New Perspectives in Archaeology,* Sally R. and Lewis R. Binford, eds. Aldine Publishing Co. Chicago.
    1964   The Hopewellian Interaction Sphere in Riverine—Western Great Lakes Culture History (pp. 85-106). Joseph Caldwell and Robert L. Hall (eds.), Hopewellian Studies, *Scientific Papers Illinois State Museum,* vol. 12, Springfield.

Thomas, Cyrus
    1887   Burial Mounds of the Northern Sections of the United States. *Bureau of American Ethnology, Annual Report* 5, Washington, D.C.
    1894   Report on the Mound Explorations of the Bureau of American Ethnology. *Bureau of American Ethnology, Annual Report* 12, Washington, D.C.

Voegelin, Carl
    1941   Internal Relationships of Siouan Languages. *American Anthropologist,* vol. 43: 246-249, Menasha.

Wedel, Mildred Mott
    1959   Oneota Sites on the Upper Iowa River. *Missouri Archaeologist,* vol. 21, nos. 2-4: 1-181, Columbia.
    1961   Indian Villages on the Upper Iowa River. *The Palimpsest,* vol 44, no. 2: 118-122, State Historical Society, Iowa City.
    1963   Note on Oneota Classification. *Wisconsin Archeologist,* vol. 44, no. 2: 118-122, Milwaukee.

Wedel, Waldo R.
1959   An Introduction to Kansas Archaeology. *Bureau of American Ethnology Bulletin* 174, Washington, D.C.

1961   *Prehistoric Man on the Great Plains.* The University of Oklahoma Press, Norman.

White, Theodore E.
1954   Observations on the Butchering Technique of Some Aboriginal Peoples. *American Antiquity,* vol. 19, no. 3: 254-256, Salt Lake City.

Willey, Gordon R.
1966   *An Introduction to American Archaeology.* vol. 1, *North and Middle America.* Prentice-Hall. Englewood Cliffs, New Jersey.

Wittry, Warren L.
1963   The Bell Site, Wn9, An Early Historic Fox Village. *Wisconsin Archeologist,* vol. 44, no. 1: 1-57, Milwaukee.

Wittry, Warren L. and David A. Baerreis
1958   Domestic Houses at Aztalan. *Wisconsin Archeologist,* vol. 39, no. 1: 62-77, Milwaukee.

Wolff, Hans
1950   Comparative Siouan. *International Journal of American Linguistics,* vol. 16: 61-66, 113-121, 168-178, Baltimore.

Wood, W. Raymond
1965   The Redbird Focus and the Problem of Ponca Prehistory. *Plains Anthropologist,* vol. 10, no. 28: 80-133, Lincoln.

10. TABLES

TABLE 1. STORAGE PITS

Storage Pit			Size				Pottery				Contents	
								Oneota				
Pit	Excavation	304 Catalogue	Total Depth (inches)	Subsoil Depth (inches)	Diameter N–S (feet)	Diameter E–W (feet)	Rims	Decorated (non-rims)	Plain Body	Woodland	Total Sherds	Total Artifacts
1	AA1	30	38	16	2.2	2.8			4		4	
2	AA1	31	36	14	3.1	3.0			2		2	
3	A4	--	25	--	--	3.4	Not Excavated					
4	A5	9	28	8	3.8	3.1		1		4	5	2
5	A5	10	31	11	3.0	3.2					None	
6	A6	11	41	18	4.1	3.4	3	21	62		86	8
7	A7	12	36	15	3.0	3.1	7	39	59		105	7
8	B3	29	40	13	3.1	2.8	1		6		7	
9	F	95	36	20	2.2	1.9					None	
10	F	94	42	20	2.6	2.4	2	1	24		27	4
11	C5	93	37	19	2.8	2.9			5		5	1
12	C6	63	32	12	2.3	2.2		3	4		7	1
13	B7	27	40	17	3.5	3.3	2	10	19		31	2
14	B8	--	18	2	2.2	2.1					None	
15	E	91	53	38	3.7	4.1			5		5	
16	d	96	29	8	3.6	3.5					None	
17	d	90	27	10	2.2	2.4					None	
18	d	89	26	10	1.3	2.2					None	
19	d	88	39	20	3.7	6.8	5		7		12	1
20	B12	34	54	27	2.6	2.0	2	2	8		12	2
21	B12	106	34	14	3.0	2.8	1		9		10	1
22	B17	--	15	--	2.4	2.0	Hearth				None	
23	B19	43	56	36	5.3	5.5	7	10	40		57	10
24	B19	42	36	15	2.8	2.5	2	7	27		36	3
25	B19	40	39	21	2.3	2.5		4	12		16	1
26	B19	41	26	4	3.1	3.3		3	6		9	
27	B19	39	36	14	3.0	3.4		3	12	1	16	
28	C21	108	43	26	4.7	3.5			5		5	
29	C21	107	45	28	3.8	3.3	2	1	33		36	5
30	C21	105	41	24	2.9	3.7			3		3	1
31	B22	65	18	--	1.2	1.6	Hearth				None	
32	B23	50	29	10	2.3	2.1	2	15	35	3	55	
33	B24	101	38	23	2.8	3.1			3		3	1
34	B24	66	22	8	2.6	2.9	1	3	52		56	
35	B24	52	40	27	3.7	4.3	1	2	23		26	
36	B23	49	30	10	2.4	2.3	1	6	20		27	
37	B24	64	33	14	2.7	2.5		5	33		38	
38	B24	--	22	9	1.3	1.2					None	
39	B24	102	42	28	4.4	2.6		2	8		10	
40	B24	53	35	23	3.0	2.8	3	10	33		46	
41	B26	54	24	10	3.3	4.1			1	2	3	1
42	B26	--	22	8	4.2	4.6					None	
43	T13	80	29	10	2.6	2.8	5	21	46		72	1
Total: all storage pits							47	169	606	10	832	52
Totals: all excavation units							91	269	787	14	1188	103
Percentage: storage pit sample							52%	57%	77%	72%	70%	50%

TABLE 2. BURIALS ATTRIBUTED TO THE WOODLAND TRADITION

Burial	Mound Association	Depth (Inches)	Catalogue – 304	Illustration Figure Number	Secondary Burial	Primary Burial	Adult	Child	No Artifacts	Notes
A	14	26	4	46	X		X		X	scattered bones, no skull.
B	14	22	5	46		(?)		X		scattered bones, fairly complete skeleton. May have been primary; later disturbed.
C	14	24	22	29	X		X		X	single isolated cranium fragment; perforated. Uncertain whether Oneota or Woodland.
D	14	20	6		X		X		X	single isolated cranium fragment.
E	14	19	D		X		(?)		X	isolated molar.
F	14	16	D		X		(?)		X	isolated long bone fragment.
G	14	16	D		X		(?)		X	isolated cranium fragment.
H	14	18	11		X		X		X	Isolated 2 molars, 1 canine.
I	none	12	D		X		(?)		X	isolated skull cut across by bulldozer.
K	none	22	D		X		X		X	bundle burial.
M	none	14	D			X	X		X	skull to west; legs and skull only, torso missing. Crushed under bulldozer.
N	50	12	45		X		X		X	isolated fragment of both mandible and skull.
O	50	10	86	47	X		X		X	long bone and skull fragments.
P	50	10	83	47		(?)	X		X	legs and skull fragments; very incomplete and no other bones present.
Q	50	16	84	47	X		X		X	2 isolated long bone fragments.
R	50	22	85	47		X	X		X	long bones of legs, partial pelvis, partial arms and skull. Extended with skull to east. Entire torso missing. Skeleton possibly rearticulated.
S	50	14	44		X		X		X	2 long bone fragments and 2 molars.

Burial B had a stone with a natural concavity; a potential artifact. D means skeletal material not catalogued.

TABLE 3. GRANT, ANKER, AND OAK FOREST ONEOTA HOUSE DIMENSIONS

House	Length	Width	Estimated floor area	Perimeter Excavated	Excavation
Grant 1	64	24	1500	180	Complete
Grant 2	65	26	1650	190	Complete
Grant 3	88	26	2200	205	Almost complete
Grant 3A	Rebuilt Wall		1950 ?	20	Complete
Grant 3B	76	26	1950	28	House 3 end stage
Grant 4	Incomplete		- - - -	40	Incomplete
Grant 5	62	26	1600	120	Incomplete
Grant 5A	Rebuilt Wall		1600	15	Complete
Grant 6	76	30	2200	165	Incomplete
Grant 7	76	20	1500	110	Incomplete
Grant 8	X	26	- - - -	20	Incomplete
Anker 1	55	13	700	130	Complete
Oak Forest 1	47.5	13.5	600	125	Complete
Oak Forest 2	25	15	350	80	Complete
Oak Forest 3	- - -	15	- - -	45	Incomplete
Oak Forest 4	27	13.8	350	82	Complete
Oak Forest 5	32	12.5	375	90	Complete
Oak Forest 6	- - -	15	- - - -	45	Incomplete
Oak Forest 7	25	12	380	75	Complete
Oak Forest 8	31	13.5	400	90	Complete

Sources for Anker and Oak Forest sites: Bluhm and Liss (1961), Bluhm and Fenner (1961). Estimated floor area is approximate, rounded off to less than length X width measurement to account for rounded ends and width variations. House line perimeter is estimated lineal length of post lines excavated and is approximate. If Grant house 3B is part of 3, the excavated perimeter would be 180 feet. All dimensions in feet.

TABLE 4. TWO SIOUAN LANGUAGE CLASSIFICATIONS

VOEGELIN CLASSIFICATION LANGUAGE GROUPS		WOLFF CLASSIFICATION LANGUAGE GROUPS	MAJOR TRIBES
MISSOURI RIVER		1. CROW-HIDATSA	CROW HIDATSA
	?	2. MANDAN	MANDAN
		3. DAKOTA	SANTEE YANKTON TETON ASSINIBOIN
	?		
MISSISSIPPI VALLEY		4. CHIWERE- WINNEBAGO	IOWAY OTO MISSOURI
			WINNEBAGO
		5. DHEGIHA	OMAHA PONCA
	?		OSAGE KANSA QUAPAW
OHIO VALLEY		6. OHIO VALLEY	TUTELO BILOXI
			OFO
EASTERN		7. CATAWBA	CATAWBA

Source: spatial expression of relationships is derived from a comparison of Voegelin (1941) and Wolff (1950). Spelling of Ioway, Chiwere, and Dhegiha changed to conform to the text.

TABLE 5. LONGHOUSES VISITED BY THE EXPLORERS

Linguistic Affiliation	Tribe	Year Visited	Month	House Cover	Visitor	House Size
Dhegiha	Quapaw	1687	July	bark	Joutel	Some large enough to hold 200 people
Dhegiha	Osage	1806	August	mats	Pike	36 to 100 feet long; 20 feet high
Dhegiha	Kansa	1811	summer	bark, mats hides	Sibley	60 feet long; 25 feet wide
"Chiwere"	Ioway	1833	April	- - - -	Maximilian	large enough for a great number
Dakota	Santee	1820	August	bark	Schoolcraft	60 feet long; 30 feet wide

Note: In addition to the explorers, later ethnographic reports record traditional use of bark covered longhouses among the Winnebago, and houses 40 feet long among the Ponca. References for the table appear in the text.

TABLE 6. BIRD FAUNA FROM TWO ILLINOIS ONEOTA SITES

Anker Site

Canada Goose	bones	Present in Illinois
Branta canadensis	1	E Feb to M Sept
Lesser Scaup*		
Ayathya affinis	1	M Mar to E Nov
Wood Duck		
Aix sponsa	1	M Mar to M Sept
Mallard		
Anas platyrhynchos	1	M Mar to E Jan

Old Forest Site

Bald Eagle		
Haliaeetus leucocephalus	1	L Mar to E Sept
Wild Turkey		
Meleagris gallopavo	3	Year round
Sandhill or Little Brown Crane		
Grus canadensis	3	E April to Unknown
Passenger Pigeon		
Ectopistes migratorius	1	L Mar to M Sept
Green Winged Teal		
Anas carolinensis	1	E Mar to E Nov

Note: Faunal remains listed in Bluhm and Liss (1961) for Anker; and Bluhm and Fenner (1961) for Oak Forest site. Seasonal presence of birds from Cooke (1888). *Lesser Scaup reads Lesser Scamp in site report, E M L abbreviation for Early, Middle, and Late.

TABLE 7. ARTIFACT FREQUENCIES

FLAKED STONE			SHAPED STONE		
Allamakee Sites	Grant Site	Group Type	Allamakee Sites	Grant Site	Group Type
(102)	(13)	Projectiles	(39)	(5)	Abrading
97	10	triangular	33	3	arrowshaft
5	0	side notched	6	1	sharpening
0	3	stemmed	ND	1	wide groove
(40)	(24)	Bifacial (knives)	(13)	(3)	Grinding
1	6	trianguloid	5	1	mano
11	1	ellipsoidal	A	1	metate
1	0	stemmed blade	A	1	thin slab
6	5	curved flake	8	0	rubbing stones
ND	7	blade fragments	(4)	(1)	Hammering
18	3	scraper knives	1	0	hammerstone
2	1	core chopper	1	0	grooved hammer
1	0	celt	2	0	chisel (?)
(79)	(42)	Unifacial (scrapers)	0	1	celt
38	7	end, ridge	(8)	(3)	Miscellaneous
23	5	end, flat	1	1	ball
ND	5	end, flake	·6	0	elbow pipe
6	8	round	1	0	monitor pipe
8	11	side scraper	0	0	catlinite tablets
ND	6	side, flake	0	1	limestone tablet
(4)	(7)	Pointed (drills)	0	1	grooved charm (?)
1	3	expanded base			
2	1	bi-pointed	SHELL ARTIFACTS		
1	0	graver	11	1	all types
ND	3	miscellaneous			

BONE ARTIFACTS			COPPER		
(67)	(4)		(25)	(1)	
13	1	scapula hoe	11	1	tubes
0	1	human cranium (drilled)	16	0	other types
10	0	tubes, beads	TRADE IRON, GLASS		
22	0	needles (all types)			
4	1	antler tips	6	0	iron
18	0	.other antler tools	Present	0	glass beads
	1	racoon *os penis*			

Allamakee sites are the combined Orr Focus artifact totals from Mildred Wedel (1959: 93-96, table 1). In some cases types have been combined. ND means not specifically described. Some listed types are not exactly comparable; see text.

TABLE 8. LANE ENCLOSURE AND GRANT POTTERY COMPARISONS

RIM DECORATION VARIETY	GRANT		LANE ENCL.	
	N	%	N	%
1. Flattened (22-35mm)	0	.0	4	1.0
2. Punctate	2	2.5	4	1.0
3. Narrow notch (1-4mm)	0	.0	97	24.3
4. Wedge notch (3-10mm)	1	1.3	106	26.4
5. Medium notch (5-14mm)	53	67.0	115	28.7
6. Wide notch (14-23mm)	12	15.2	5	1.3
7. Indeterminate	1	1.3	20	5.0
8. Interior notch	10	12.7	16	4.0
9. Exterior notch	0	.0	7	1.8
10. Undecorated	0	.0	26	6.5
OTHER ATTRIBUTES	GRANT		LANE ENCL.	
	N	%	N	%
Leaching				
none	70	6.0	141	70.5
medium	184	15.7	36	18.0
extreme	920	78.3	23	11.5
Trailed Lines				
narrow (under 3.0mm)	118	38.3	66	74.2
medium (3.0-3.5mm)	164	52.3	20	22.5
broad (over 3.5mm)	26	8.4	3	3.3
Punctates				
border areas	15	100.0	0	0
filled areas	0	.0	17	100.0
Rim Height				
short (under 3.0cm)	17	34.0	18	10.8
medium (3.0-5.0cm)	29	58.0	101	60.5
tall (over 5.0cm)	4	8.0	48	28.7

11. ILLUSTRATIONS

1. HARTLEY TERRACE VICINITY, simplified from the current U.S.G.S. preliminary unpublished topographic sheet with sites added.

2. NORRIS SKETCH OF SITES, from Thomas 1894, plate 5, with larger identifying letters added. A. Lane Enclosure. B. Lane Mounds. C. Brown's Hill mounds. D. Hartley Fort. E. Unlocated enclosure. F. Unlocated stone burial chamber. Enlarged views of A and F appear in Thomas. The Little Iowa River is Upper Iowa River and the north arrow should point approximately 40 degrees east of its recorded position. The terrace outlines are inaccurate; the connection or saddle running south to the Owl, a second hill, not being shown. Compare with figures 1 and 3.

3. HARTLEY TERRACE SITES, redrawn from Orr 1963, vol. 1: 69, with 1970 additions and site designations.

4. RADIOCARBON CHRONOLOGY, from Geochron Laboratory 1970 determinations of charcoal samples. Sample numbers listed in Chapter 1.

5. 1970 EXCAVATION PLAN, showing all excavation and provenience units at the Grant site except T14 parallel and south of T13, and T15 extended south. T trenches were bulldozer cuts mainly beyond the village periphery. Features, generally storage pits, are numbered sequentially. X-series burials are labeled alphabetically. Plans and air photographs are available in the The University of Iowa Map Room for more detailed relocation of excavations. The bench mark (BM) is an iron rod set flush in concrete near the northeast fence corner. The complete T trench series appears in figure 23.

6. WEST HOUSE AREA, located on previous plan, shows the relative size of all post molds drawn to scale, but uniformly enlarged slightly. The circled numbered areas are storage pits. The X-series burials are numbered alphabetically. A and B reference points on the left edge of the west house area divide the plan into three segments, enlarged views appearing in figures 8, 9, and 10. The group of figures 6-10 is derived from a single drawing described under figure 8.

7. IDENTIFICATION OF STRUCTURES, west house area is the same plan of the post molds shown in the plan 6, but storage pit numbers, burial letters, and segment reference letters A and B are omitted. The lines showing the probable structures are added, and numbered sequentially, each structure is discussed in the text and summarized in table 3. This illustration is paired with figure 6 in order to provide both interpretive and non-interpretive views of the post lines.

8. SOUTH SECTION, west house area, is an enlarged view of the plan shown in figure 6. The segment runs from the bottom to reference point A. Storage pits are numbered within edge outlines, and X identifies burial letter designations. The larger numbers, 1 to 3B are post lines identified as house walls in figure 7. Each post mold diameter is given in inches. The relative size of all post molds

is drawn to the same scale, but uniformly enlarged slightly relative to the plan scale. The post mold diameters represent averages to the nearest inch, being approximations. A common base negative was used for all figures 6 through 10. It was made from an unlettered redrawing of the original field plans, scaled 2 feet: 1 inch, with different kinds of identifying information added to each figure. Thus, this group of figures is internally uniform and consistent in representing the post lines. The scale in feet runs from 0 to 40 plus. Since the house axis and excavation lies SE-NW, this figure might more accurately be identified as the southeast section, a designation not used because no southwest section is present.

9.   CENTRAL SECTION, west house area, is an enlarged view of the plan shown in figure 6, the segment lying between reference letters A and B. Identifying numbers, letters and post mold diameters are explained in figure 8. The scale in feet runs from minus 50 to 80 plus, having an overlap with figures 8 and 10.

10.   NORTH SECTION, west house area, is an enlarged view of the plan in figure 6, the segment being located from reference point B to the top of the figure. The extreme left margin of the west house area excavation is not shown. Identifying numbers, letters and post mold diameters are explained in figure 8. The scale in feet runs from minus 90 to 130 plus.

11.   EAST HOUSE AREA, a scale reduction from the redrawing of the field plans originally having the scale of 2 feet: 1 inch. Storage pit edges are identified, by number, and X-burial series by letter. The east house area is located on the excavation plan, figure 5. The edge of the Lane Mound 50 is difficult to identify precisely because field cultivation leveled the mound. The somewhat spread and irregular margins are located approximately on the excavation plan, figure 5, and the smaller original outline is suggested in figure 23. The possible east wall of the house seems to lie parallel to the west wall, and runs through storage pits 32, 36, 37, and 39, which obscured the post line. If this is correct, the house width is 30 feet, the maximum found in the west house area. The west house wall shows a redundancy of posts which may represent the double framework characteristic of bark construction. Since no post line appeared west of storage pit 23, the house appears to lie over the hearth, feature 31. This entire east house area is the most logical place within the site to expand future excavations.

12.   INTERIOR POLE FRAMEWORKS, from Bushnell 1922, plates 18a and 32a, show two major variations in form. The Osage (upper) has three internal centered posts supporting the ridge, construction features which seem to be survivals from the larger houses of the past. The Fox framework (lower) lacks interior supports and ridge, and is the construction best adapted to small arch spans.

13.   OJIBWA LONGHOUSE AND MAT, the framework lacks interior posts, and both the great width and height of the Mississippi River lodges. The example is from Ritchie 1965: 283, and the National Museum of Canada. The house mat, incompletely shown, provides detail on one form of edge sewing, and is from Bushnell 1922, plate 12b.

14.   WINNEBAGO BARK LODGES, have porch extensions, a common feature. The standing forked posts of an abandoned lodge show the usual way to support the transverse porch, side wall and ridge poles. The example (upper) is from Radin 1923, plate 19a. The central porch (lower) between two separate lodges might be confused with a single archaeological structure, although the poles are farther apart and thicker than curved lodge poles. The illustration is from Bushnell 1922, plate 37.

15.   WINNEBAGO BARK LODGES, show patching with reed mats and canvas, and details of the exterior pole framework. Illustrated by Radin 1923, plate 18a, b.

16.   IOWAY BARK LODGE AND IROQUOIS BENCH, from Plank 1908: 315 (upper), and Morgan 1851 opp. 3. The Ioway example has a porch, here unroofed, and the typical exterior pole framework. The purpose of poles resting along one side is unclear, but they may merely be stored in that position until further use, since they provide no structural or sheathing support. The stylized Iroquois lodge bench is inaccurate, but shows the family compartment. Cruder versions may have appeared in the Mississippi Valley lodges.

17.   WINNEBAGO MAT COVERED LODGES, from Bushnell 1922, plate 36, show that this type of house sheath requires no exterior framework except horizontal stringers to bind the mat edges to the interior frame. The mats are larger and conform better than bark to the interior framework, making vertical exterior posts unnecessary.

18.   SANTEE AND IROQUOIS BARK LODGES, from Bushnell 1922, plate 22a (upper), and Morgan 1851 opp. 3, show some parallels in construction. Both have gable construction, front entryway, and the exterior pole framework binding the sheathing to the interior frame. The Santee houses are the smaller form drawn in the 1850s, while the Iroquois example is also nineteenth century, long after the longhouse had fallen into disuse. Note the extensive use of house platforms by the Santee.

19.   SAUK SUMMER LODGES, show exterior bark framework, and gable construction with front entryway. The Sauk example from Bushnell 1922, plate 19 (upper) has a somewhat curved or bowed dormer wall and the seated Indians suggest a ridge height of about 15 feet; and a house width approaching the Grant houses. The length is much less. This may be a reasonably close approximation of the larger prehistoric lodges and is used as a pattern in the Grant reconstruction in figure 25. The Sauk example, with straight dormer sides and uncovered lower walls is not a true residence, and shows the effect of increased later modifications (lower). It is illustrated in Skinner 1925, plate 13, figure 1.

20.   SAUK SUMMER LODGE, from Rebok 1900: 34, is the gable bark covered type, with exterior porch and with front entryway. The exterior framework is partially masked by the gabled front porch or shed. The width is close to the

Grant examples and the estimated height is over twelve feet allowing for perspective foreshortening.

21.   OMAHA AND KANSA LODGES; a characteristic plains village settlement pattern is illustrated by the Omaha (upper), who have arrived from their winter camp and reset their tipis, but have not yet moved into summer earth lodges. The Kansa house (lower) is a clearly transitional type, showing the change from the earlier larger houses to bark covered copies of earth lodges. Examples from Bushnell 1922, plates 27 and 31.

22.   ILLINOIS ONEOTA HOUSE PLANS, show narrow but long lodges. The Anker site house plan (left), is from Bluhm and Liss 1961: 100, and the fewer posts in the lower third suggest an addition. The Oak Forest house from Bluhm and Fenner 1961: 142, also suggests an addition in the lower quarter. The paired, margin posts suggest bark sheathing. Despite the narrow width both houses have central posts for ridge support, like the Osage framework, figure 12 (upper). The multiple central supports suggest repeated rebuilding and this is particularly evident in the Anker house. These plans have been redrawn to the same scale, and are simplified from the originally published drawings.

23.   GRANT SETTLEMENT PATTERN is projected from the excavation plan, figure 5. Main trenches are A-A, B-B, and T series. The discussion in the text, chapter 5, explains the basis for drawing the village boundary and it is estimated approximately along the north and southeast sections. Houses 2, 6, and 8 follow patterns designated as structures in figures 7 and 11. House ? is projected in an unexcavated area. The X-X lines are the trench in the linear mound ascribed to Norris. No house evidence was found in the village center along the B-B line and no houses appeared in the A line.

24.   ONEOTA SETTLEMENT PATTERNS, all four site excavations redrawn to the same scale suggest that small Oneota settlements about an acre in size may be a typical residential pattern in some regions. The Lane Enclosure settlement is projected from the 1880s Norris map, Orr's extensive excavations in the 1930s and the 1970 re-investigation. The stockade-embankment has an overlapping entryway, with numerous interior storage pits, and an open central area. The house type is unknown, since the 1970 work was at the north embankment. The Grant settlement is a simplification of the plan in figure 23. The Oak Forest settlement is derived from the site map in Bluhm and Fenner, 1961: 138, and the Anker house redrawn from Bluhm and Liss 1961: 93.

25.   GRANT BARK HOUSES, drawn by Frank Sindelar, shows the curved ended, gabled bark lodge type with exterior framework, derived from figure 19 (upper), in the relative positions of Houses 2 and 6 looking north to the edge of the terrace. The drying of bark slabs separated by poles is reported by Skinner (1926) for the Ioway. There should be more structural wall frame poles, and there is no archaeological evidence of deer butchering at the village. The placement of the doorways on the side rather than the ends is arbitrary. They occur

on gable ends of Sauk and Santee lodges, and from the description seem to have been located on the end of the Winnebago ten-fire lodges. No clear statement occurs for the Kansa. The presence of end platforms in the Quapaw bark lodges may have made a side entryway practical. The Osage mat lodges had a platform at one end and side doorways are specifically described. Doorways are usually at the ends of the smaller bark lodges previously illustrated for the Winnebago and Ioway, figures 14, 16.

26.   GRANT MAT HOUSES, drawn by Frank Sindelar, show the curving variety of side framework, and these are derived in part from the Winnebago mat covered lodges illustrated in figure 17. The houses are 2 and 6 looking north. More Indians will be needed to raise the pole being placed in position.

27.   STONE AND BONE TOOLS: A. natural concavity associated with burial X-B, 304-5. B. broken sandstone metate 304-70. C. fragment of discoidal abrading tablet 304-75. D. bison scapula hoe, incomplete, 304-96. E. narrow grooved abrader 304-9. F. celt 304-69. G. sandstone mano fragment 304-87.

28.   STONE AND BONE TOOLS: A. worked antler tip from the Lane Enclosure comparable to a more incomplete specimen from the Grant site 310-70. B. fragment of sandstone arrowshaft abrader 304-38. C. stemmed point from post hole, west house area 304-75. D-E. stemmed points from storage pit 23, both 304-109. F. ellipsoidal knife 304-2. G. shell fragment with edge notching 304-12.

29.   MISCELLANEOUS OBJECTS: A. human cranium with perforation 304-22. B. small complete amulet, limestone, with edge notching and incised design 304-27. C. fragment of small grooved ornament, possibly earspool 304-27. D. stone ball 304-92. E. daub specimen 304-21. F. tubular copper ornament 304-75.

30.   FLAKED STONE TOOLS: A-B. core tools 304-40, 103. C. drill 304-75. D. scraper knife 304-47. E-G. curved flake knives 304-12, 19, 9. H. flake end scraper 304-20.

31.   FLAKED STONE TOOLS: A and E. expanded base drills 304-40, 109. B. bi-pointed drill with broken tips 304-67. C and F. miscellaneous drills 304-11, 12. D. sliver of broken side scraper 304-12. G-L. triangular projectile points, some broken 304-58, 34, 28, 74, 94, 11.

32.   FLAKED STONE TOOLS: A-E. round scrapers 304-54, 52, 72, 109, 67. F-I. ridge end scraper 304-110, 52, 107, 52. J-K. flake end scraper 304-109, 58. L. flat end scraper 304-37.

33.   FLAKED STONE TOOLS: A-D. side scrapers 304-16, 59, 77, 101. Specimen C is also a flat end scraper. E-F. triangular knives 304-72,77.

34.   GRANT AND LANE ENCLOSURE RIMS: representational rim decoration traits. Grant A-C, Lane Enclosure D-H. A. punctates. B. medium notches. C. wide notches. Compare with Lane traits: D. flattened. E. interrupted notches. F. narrow notches. G. medium notches. H. wedge or fingernail. Drawn from specimens University Archaeological Laboratory.

35.   GRANT ONEOTA RIMS: A. 304-12. B. 304-80. C. 304-88. D. 304-72. E. 304-33.

36.   GRANT ONEOTA RIMS: A. 304-87. B. 304-34. C. 304-109. D. 304-11. E. 304-12. F. 304-60. G. 304-37.

37.   GRANT ONEOTA RIMS: A. 304-80. B. 304-82. C. 304-106. D. 304-88. E. 304-107. F. 304-72.

38.   GRANT ONEOTA RIMS WITH HANDLES: A. 304-80. B. 304-87. C. 304-88. D. 304-94. E. 304-32. F. 304-109. G. 304-58.

39.   GRANT ONEOTA DECORATED BODYSHERDS: A. 304-79. B. 304-79. C. 304-80. D. 304-54. E. 304-12.

40.   GRANT ONEOTA DECORATED BODYSHERDS: A. 304-25. B. 304-38. C. 304-8. D. 304-93. E. 304-12. F. 304-38. G. 304-40. H. 304-1. I. 304-12. J. 304-26.

41.   GRANT ONEOTA DECORATED BODYSHERDS: A. 304-50. B. 304-12. C. 304-12. D. 304-19. E. 304-26. F. 304-25. G. 304-11. H. 304-11.

42.   WOODLAND POT, Lane Farm Cord Impressed 304-73, unrestored.

43.   GRANT AND LANE PROFILES, Lane Enclosure rims A-N illustrate representative variations in container forms from the Lane Enclosure. G is a deep bowl and H is a bottle. Grant rims O-Z illustrate representative containers. No deep bowls or bottles appeared.

44.   NORRIS MOUND TRENCH, Mound 14, B trench showing refilled ditch attributed to Colonel Norris, 1882, looking northwest (lower). View of the same feature in trench B 1-5, looking west (upper).

45.   FIREPLACE, feature 22, trench B-17, looking north (upper), and the same feature seen from above.

46.   WOODLAND SECONDARY BURIALS, burials in linear mound 14 attributed to the Woodland Tradition. Burial A, secondary, adult, trench A-4, facing south (upper). Burial B, secondary, adult and child, trench A-3, with natural concavity (lower). This specimen also appears in figure 27A, and is the only associated object found with any burial.

47.   WOODLAND INCOMPLETE BURIALS, attributed to the Woodland Tradition but lacking associated artifacts. Burial R, incomplete, supine, east house area, looking south (lower). Burial R, B, P (left to right), with the few incomplete bones of burial O, on pedestal in foreground, looking south (lower).

48.   EXPLORATORY TRENCHES, cutting T series test trenches with a bulldozer south of the excavations, looking west (upper). Cache pits 4 and 5, hand excavated trench A-5, looking northwest (lower).

49.   INITIAL VIEWS OF HOUSE LINES. (upper) West house area, C trench, looking southwest. These posts formed the overlapping west walls of Houses 2 and 3, and part of the east wall of House 7. After further clearing additional post molds in this line were identified. (lower) Two house lines crossed at a

right angle initially appearing to be a single square structure, later identified as House walls 3 and 5. Trench B-7 and pit 13, looking east. Reference maps figures 5, 6, 7, and 10. Figure 51 lower, shows this same area after complete clearing.

50.   CLEARING HOUSE FLOORS. Initial view of the double row of post molds, house lines 3, 3A, square C-9, looking east (upper). The same house lines, lower left foreground, after the houses were more completely exposed, looking southwest (lower).

51.   WEST HOUSE AREA. The square corner formed by the wall lines in the center foreground with pit 13, were separate structures, identified as Houses 3 and 5. A preliminary photograph appears in figure 49 lower. All house ends identified had rounded, or flattened rounded ends, square corners being absent. (Lower) General view of the west house area, looking southwest.

52.   WEST HOUSE AREA showing complete excavation after rains. (upper) looking southeast. (lower) looking northwest. Note the separation of House 1 and 2 walls in the left foreground.

53.   LANE ENCLOSURE POTTERY, Allamakee Trailed type, shows finer lines, punctate filled triangle motifs, and narrower notches compared with Grant type pottery. Representative sherds: A. 310-4. B. 310-67. C. 310-2. D. 310-117. E. 310-30. F. 310-76. G. 310-123.

54.   LANE ENCLOSURE POTTERY, Allamakee Trailed type, representative sherds: A. 310-23. B. 310-136. C. 310-121. D. 310-63. E. 310-38. F. 310-8. G. 310-142. H. 310-136.

NOTE: The small grooved ornament, possibly an earspool, illustrated in figure 29 C, appears to be a unique specimen. It has been identified by G. R. McCormick, Department of Geology, as probably a quartz crystal nodule, purposefully ground and then coated with hematite. At some time subsequent to grinding and coating it was heated which caused the hematite to spread very evenly over the crystalline surface, and which also caused the quartz crystals to warp and lose sharp edges. Approximately one-third of the specimen is missing.

1.   HARTLEY TERRACE VICINITY

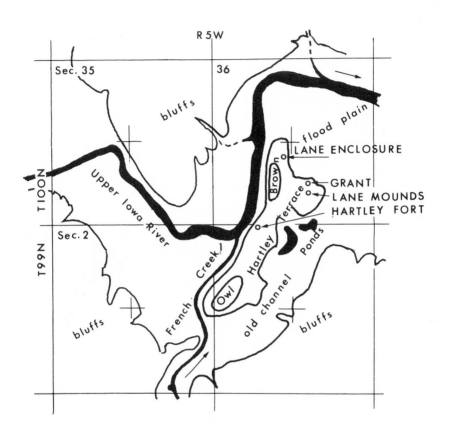

2. NORRIS SKETCH OF SITES

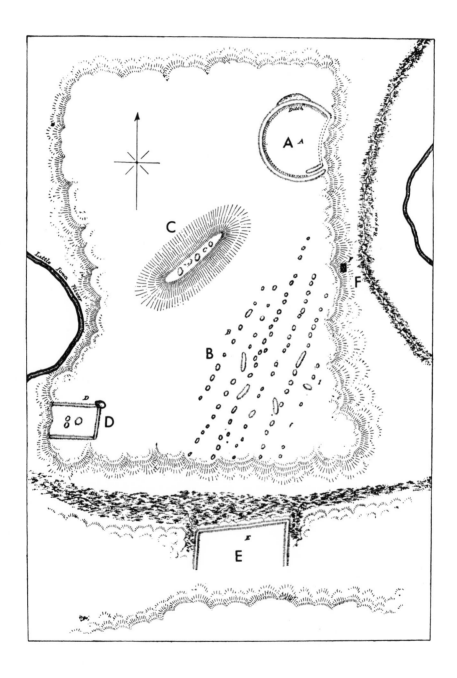

3.   HARTLEY TERRACE SITES

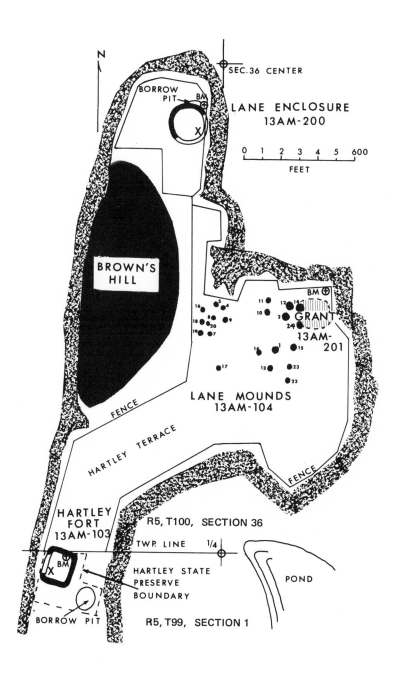

4.   RADIOCARBON CHRONOLOGY

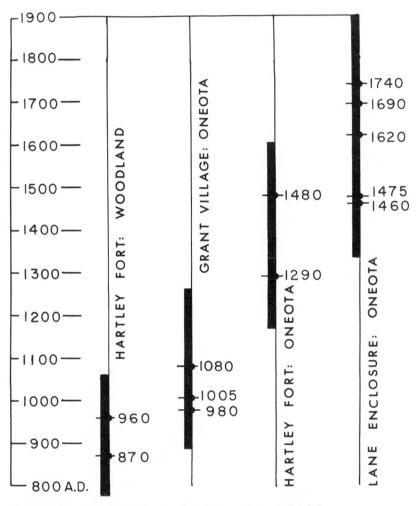

CARBON 14 DATES ± 85 TO 180 YEARS
BARS: MAXIMUM ± PER SERIES SAMPLES

5.   1970 EXCAVATION PLAN

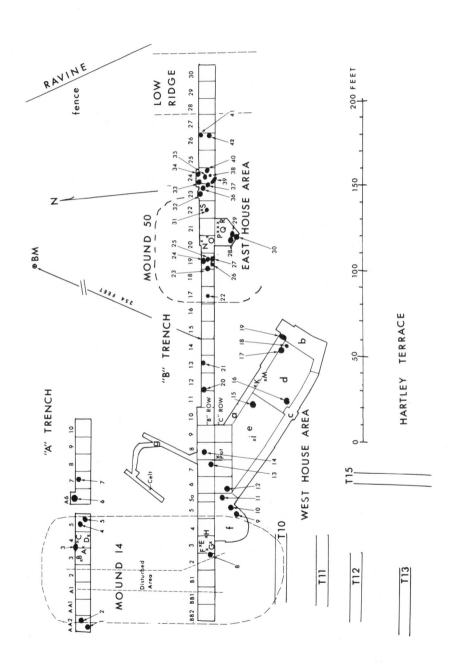

6.   WEST HOUSE AREA

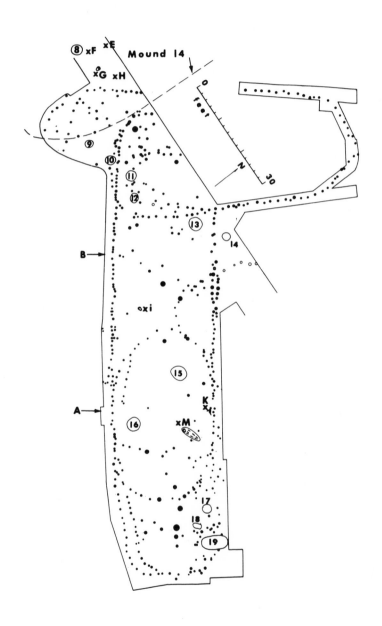

7.   IDENTIFICATION OF STRUCTURES

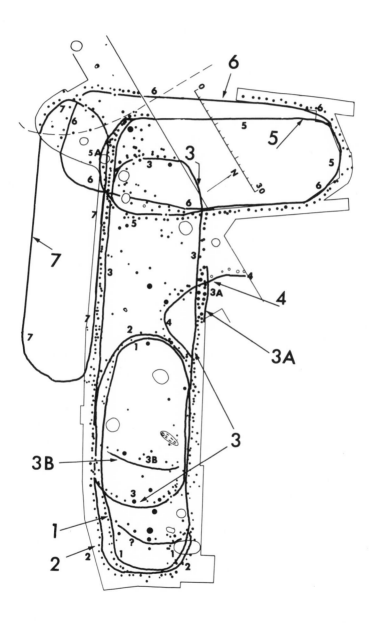

8.   **SOUTH SECTION**

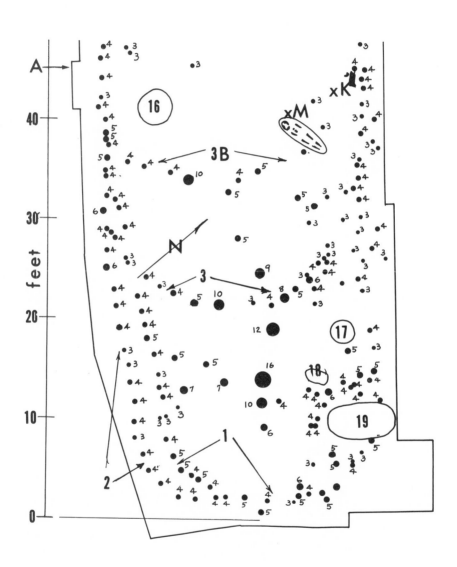

9.   CENTRAL SECTION

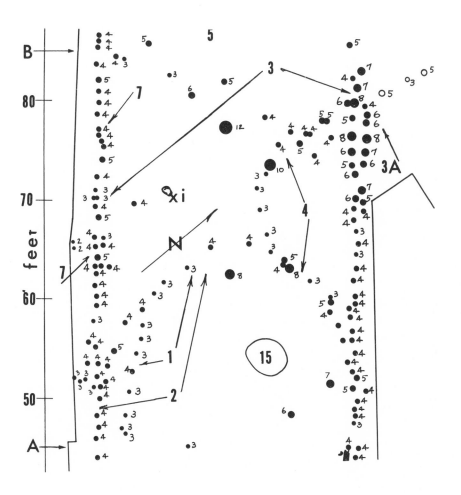

10.   **NORTH SECTION**

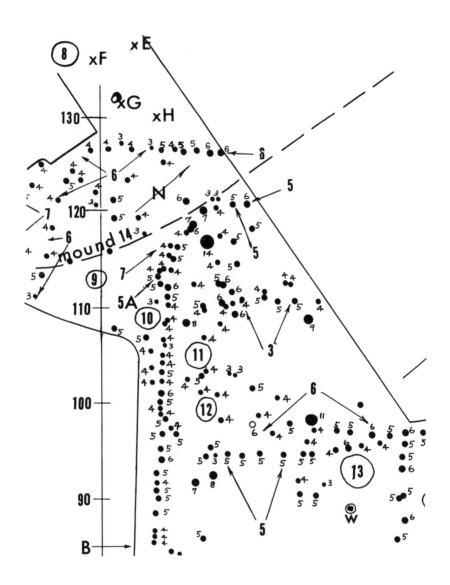

11.   EAST HOUSE AREA

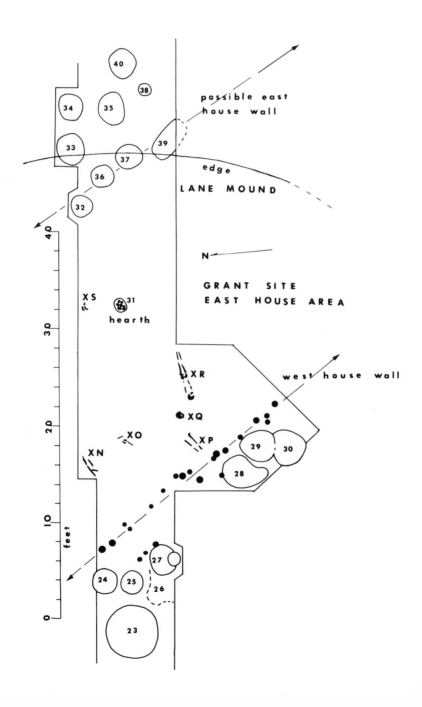

12.   INTERIOR POLE FRAMEWORKS

13.   OJIBWA LONGHOUSE AND MAT

14.   WINNEBAGO BARK LODGES

15.   WINNEBAGO BARK LODGES

16.   **IOWAY BARK LODGE AND
        IROQUOIS BENCH**

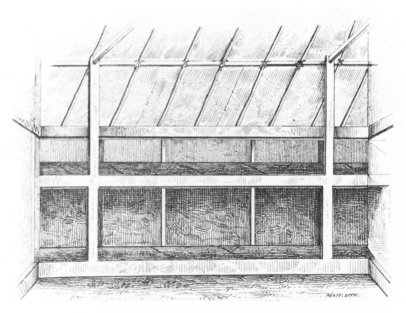

17.   WINNEBAGO MAT COVERED LODGES

18.   SANTEE AND IROQUOIS BARK LODGES

19.   **SAUK SUMMER LODGES**

20.   SAUK SUMMER LODGE

21.   OMAHA AND KANSA LODGES

22.   **ILLINOIS ONEOTA HOUSE PLANS**

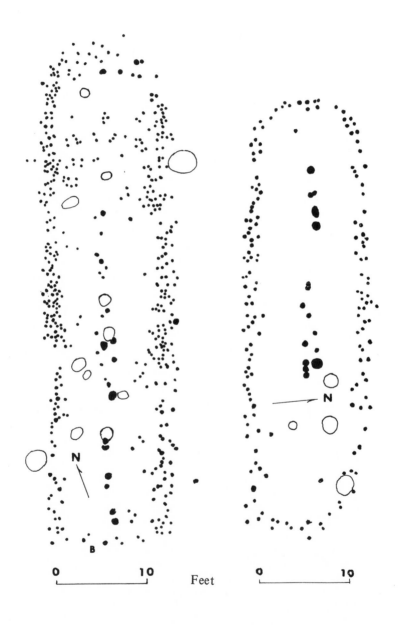

0   10   Feet   0   10

23.   GRANT SETTLEMENT PATTERN

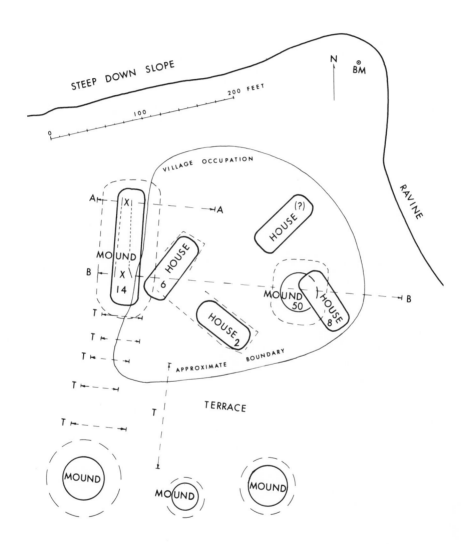

24.   ONEOTA SETTLEMENT PATTERNS

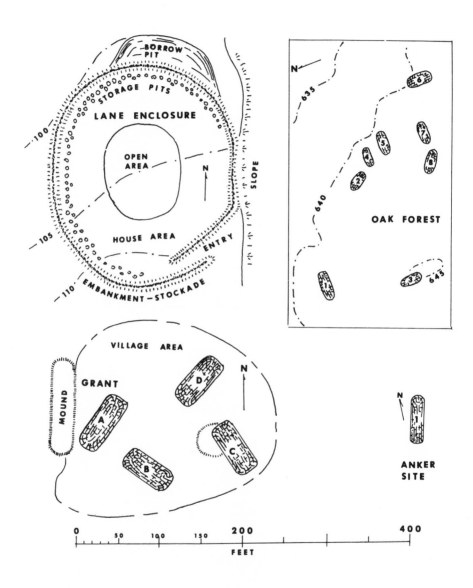

25.   GRANT BARK HOUSES

26.   GRANT MAT HOUSES

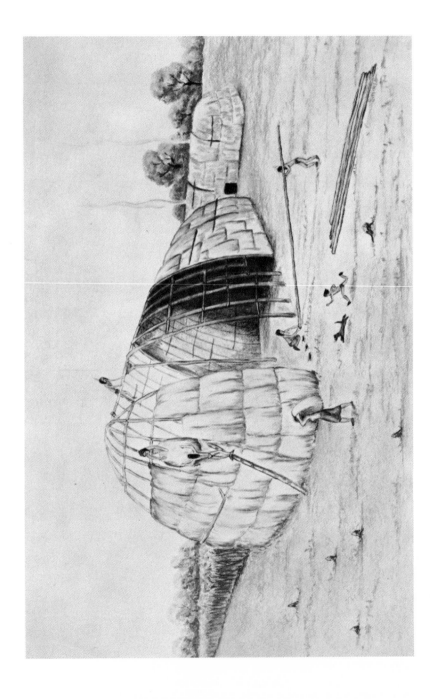

27.   STONE AND BONE TOOLS

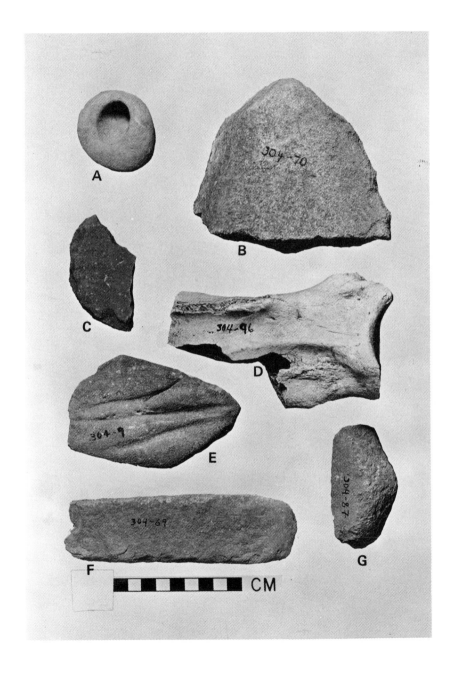

28.   **STONE AND BONE TOOLS**

29.   **MISCELLANEOUS OBJECTS**

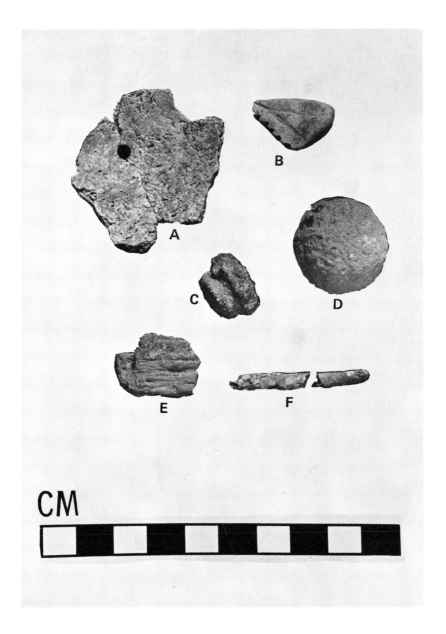

30.   **FLAKED STONE TOOLS**

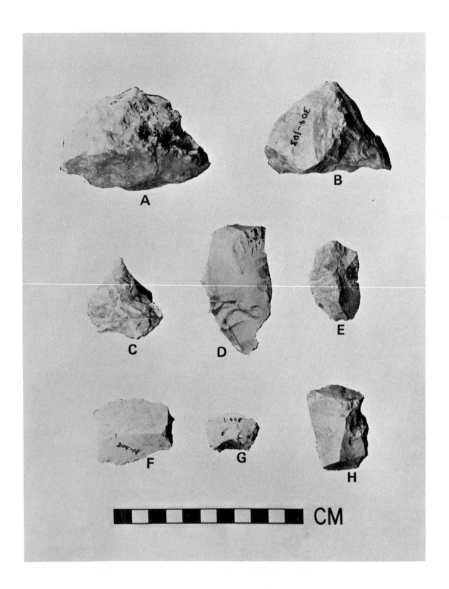

31.   FLAKED STONE TOOLS

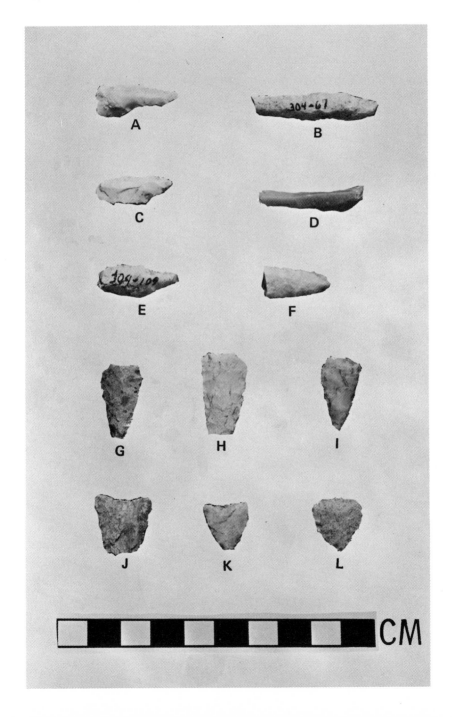

32.   FLAKED STONE TOOLS

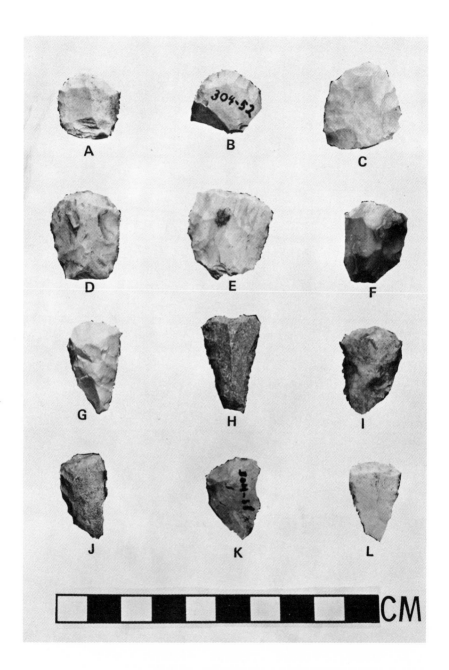

33.   FLAKED STONE TOOLS

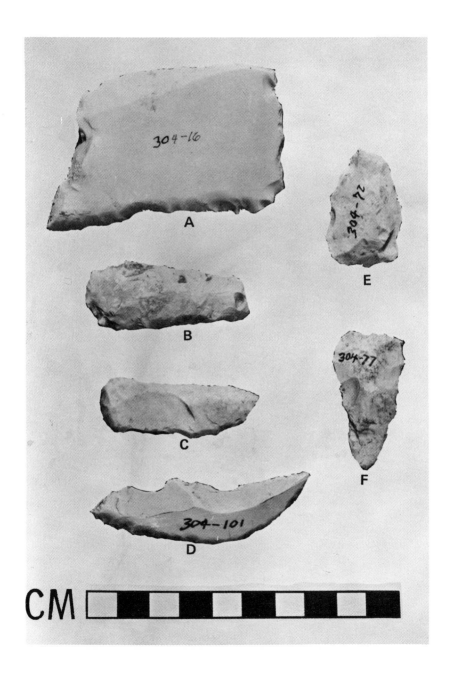

34.   GRANT AND LANE RIMS

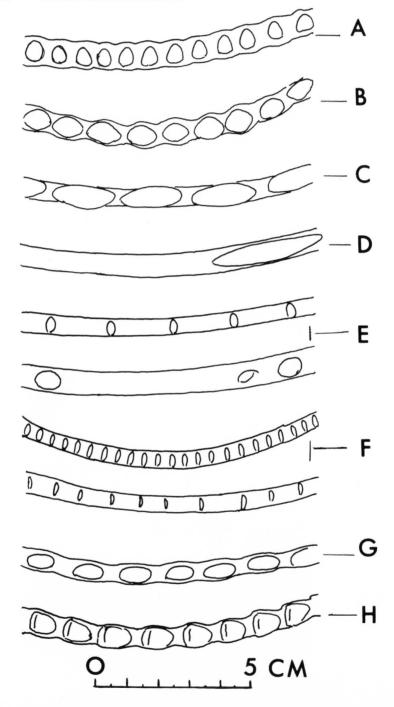

35.   GRANT RIMS

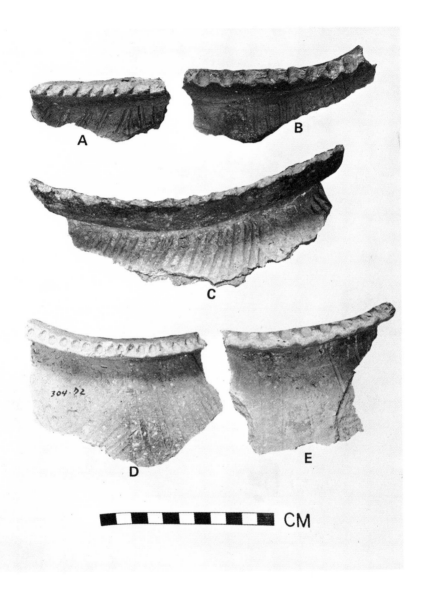

36.   GRANT RIMS

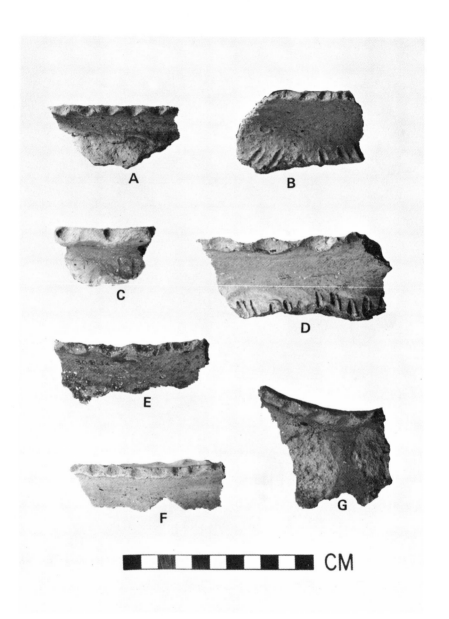

37.   **GRANT RIMS**

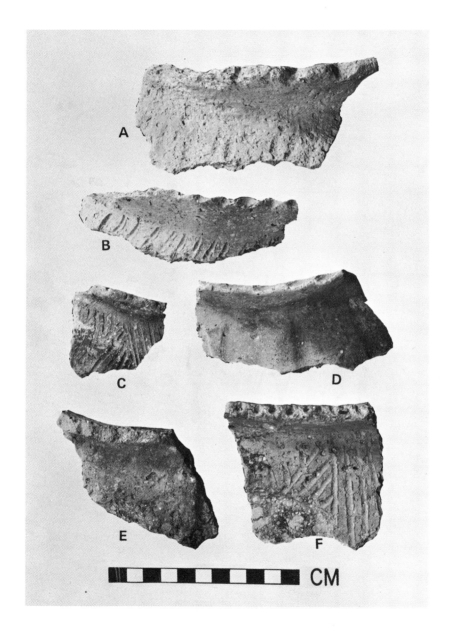

38.   GRANT RIMS

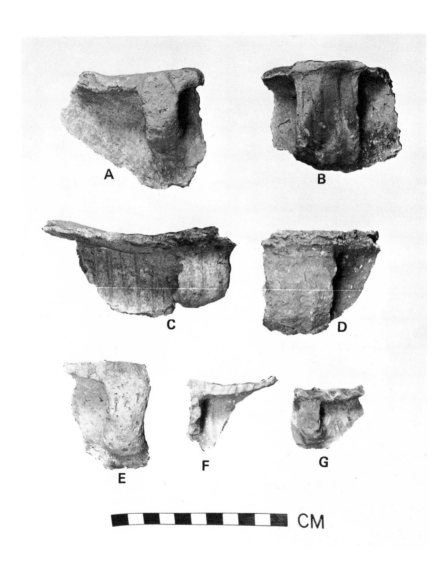

39.   **GRANT BODYSHERDS**

40.   GRANT BODYSHERDS

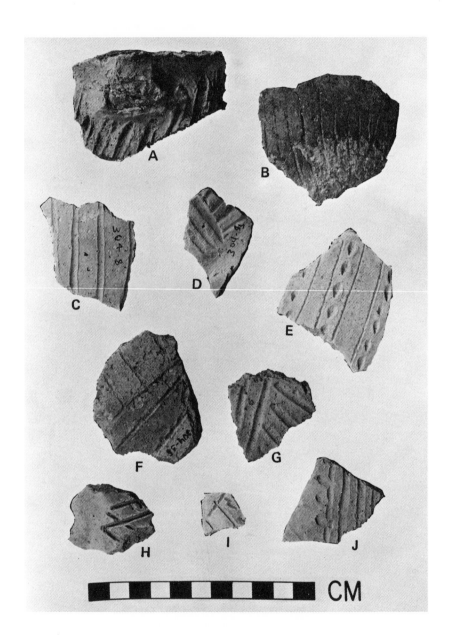

41.   GRANT BODYSHERDS

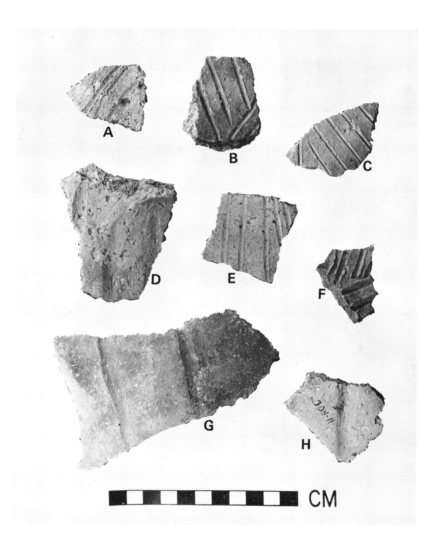

42.   WOODLAND POT

43.   GRANT AND LANE PROFILES

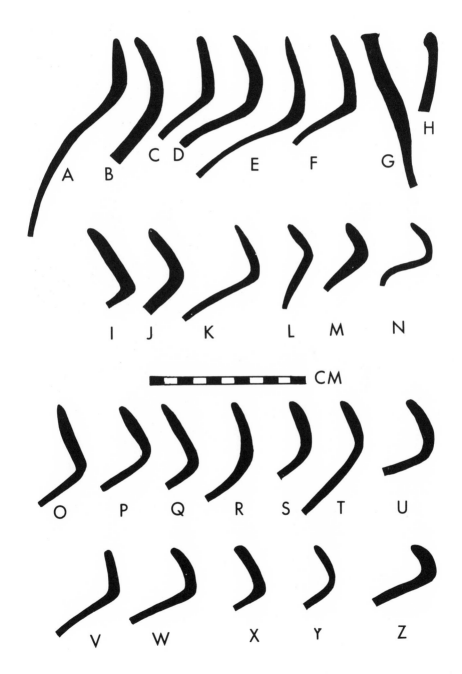

44.   NORRIS MOUND TRENCH

45.   FIREPLACE

46.   WOODLAND SECONDARY BURIALS

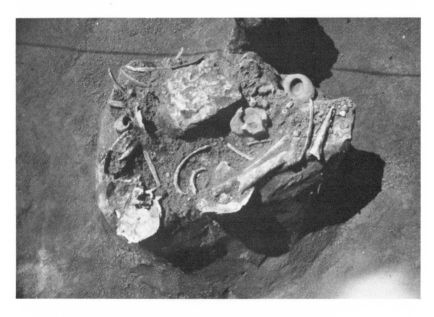

47.   WOODLAND INCOMPLETE BURIALS

48.   EXPLORATORY TRENCHES

49.   INITIAL VIEWS OF HOUSE LINES

50.   CLEARING HOUSE FLOORS

51.   WEST HOUSE AREA

52.   WEST HOUSE AREA

53.   **LANE ENCLOSURE POTTERY**

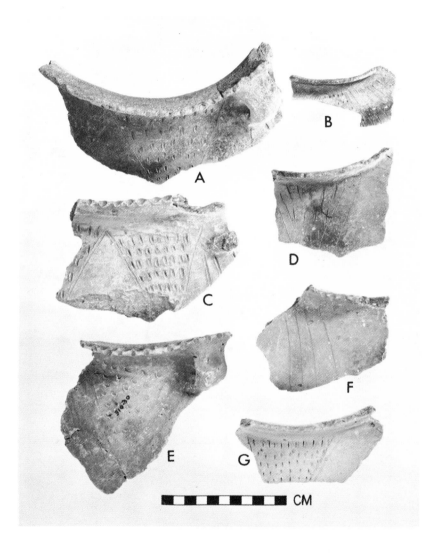

54.   LANE ENCLOSURE POTTERY

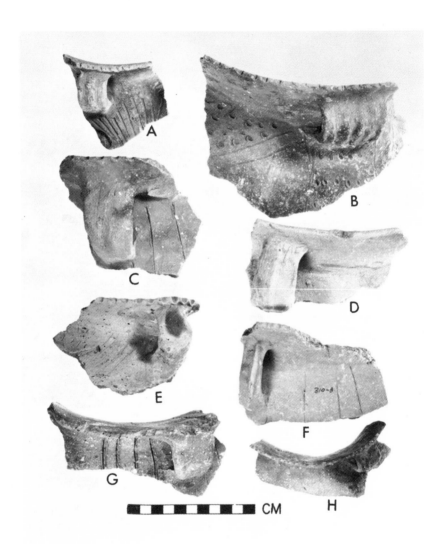

12. COMMENTARY

By DAVID A. BAERREIS*

Since others more experienced in problems of Oneota ceramic classification and cultural taxonomy will doubtless elaborate on these points, I shall confine my comments to the house complex which is clearly one of the novel features of the Grant site.

It is useful to see the extensive survey of house types occupied during the historic period by the linguistic relatives of the Grant site people, as well as those used by their neighbors. Yet while the direct historical approach and ethnographic analogy are powerful tools, we may also profit from historical continuities in the general region. The description of the Middle Woodland component houses and the comparative survey of house types found in the Summer Island site report by David S. Brose (1970) would have been a useful point of departure. I also find David Brose's analysis of the number of occupants of a house in terms of the square feet of floor space that each individual occupant requires appealing in methodology. Using somewhat different sets of data, he derives means of 28.0 and 35.4 square feet of floor space per occupant during the historic period. Based on Table 3 in McKusick's report, the average house at the Grant site would have 1,800 square feet of floor space and thus each should contain either 50 or 64 occupants. If four houses were occupied at one time, this would give us a population for the village of 200 or 250 persons. Thus from a slightly different approach, we confirm the estimate by McKusick of a village size of 200 but suggest it might perhaps have been slightly larger (250) rather than probably being on the smaller side.

Some consideration might be given to the kind of field evidence that would support one or the other of the interpretations in regard to a rounded or a gabled form of roof. In structures of the width indicated at the Grant site, poles of considerable thickness would be needed to span that space and still allow adequate head room if a rounded roof were present. Bending such poles would exert very considerable pressure at the base in the posthole, the force being directed outward from the interior of the house. Surely this pressure would have some effect on the shape of the post mold and would produce occasional structural failure with the posts springing outward as a consequence of the high degree of force. Given the time pressure under which this field excavation and indeed the average field excavation operates, it is understandable that more postholes were not sectioned. However, this might be a crucial point for future excavations to give us essential data for architectural reconstruction. McKusick mentions (p.15) that burned stones were wedged into the postholes to strengthen the set of the

---

*Professor of Anthropology, University of Wisconsin, Madison, Wisconsin.

post. Was this primarily on the outer margin? This is the critical area if the pos.s are bent, though this is not the case if we are dealing with vertical walls and a gable roof.

On the ethnohistoric side, one additional reference which is illuminating is the account of Le Sueur's *Voyage Up the Mississippi in 1699-1700* (Shea 1861). Here we learn that Le Sueur established Fort L'Huiller on Blue River (Mankato or Blue Earth River). Shortly thereafter, groups of eastern Sioux (Mantantous or Mantantons) quickly constructed houses about the fort and we are told that "on the 1st of December the Mantantons invited Mr. Le Sueur to a great banquet; four of their cabins had been thrown into one, in which there were a hundred men seated around, each with his platter before him" (*ibid:* 109). Whether these skin covered dwellings were of a tipi or wigwam shape is not indicated in the narrative, but we know that similar expansions in size could occur in the bark covered lodge. Temporary expansion of the size of a house to accommodate a large feast might well create archaeological traces which suggest extensive repair of decayed house walls had taken place. Does the rather limited amount of refuse also suggest that much of the building activity at the Grant site could be of this character, rather than long sustained activity?

Further support for the unusual character of the houses at the Grant site is provided by house structures at three Oneota sites not included in the comparative survey. Excavations carried out at the Dixon site (13WD-8) on the Little Sioux River in east central Woodbury County, Iowa, in 1964 revealed the pattern of a roughly rectangular structure at least thirty feet in length and about eight feet in width (Harvey 1971 MS:114). Since the east end of the structure had been removed by the construction of a gravel road, the length is a minimum figure. The post molds of the Dixon site house suggest a simple and irregular structure, this being also true of the indications of a house recovered at the Crescent Bay Hunt Club Site (47JE-244) in Jefferson County, Wisconsin, on the shores of Lake Koshkonong. The post molds for this house suggested a nearly square structure, lacking central supports or evidence of a fire basin, with dimensions of approximately eleven to twelve feet on the sides. Finally, Guy E. Gibbon (1969 MS) in his restudy of the Walker-Hooper site (47GL-65), one of the key sites of the Grand River Phase of Oneota in Green Lake County, Wisconsin, recovered the remains of two long, oval houses. The first measured thirty-one feet by ten and the second twenty feet by eleven. In both instances although the house floor was clearly defined, the pattern of posts around the margin lacked regularity. The presence of single firepits in these houses as well as their sizes would seem to indicate that individual houses for single families are a not infrequent attribute of Oneota.

By ALFRED W. BOWERS*

Researchers working in sites along the northern and eastern periphery of the territorial limits of Middle Mississippian settlements where intercultural exchanges with peoples of Woodland cultures had occurred and new traditions developed should take note that along the margins of the Prairie and Plains Vegetative Zones a third tradition, the Hunting tradition, had to be reckoned with in searching out the origins of the Middle Missouri tradition. Because of the vitality and rapid spread of Middle Mississippian, Griffin's (1960) hypothesis that early Oneota Aspect as a group would have rectangular Middle Mississippian wattle and daub houses was logical even though evidence at the Grant Oneota village later indicated bark or mat coverings instead. When so many variables are involved, including the heavy emphasis of Middle Mississippians toward gardening and large settlements, one might assume that the Plains rectangular lodge gardening complex would be strongly Middle Mississippian oriented but in the Great Plains this is not so.

Heretofore the factors of natural resources, physiography, and climate—to mention a few variables—have too often not been given appropriate consideration when searching for the origins of new traditions. Scholars concerned with the origin of the Oneota traditions, it seems to me, have encountered many of the same problems those researching "origins" of the Great Plains Middle Missouri tradition of rectangular lodges on the Missouri River have had to take into account. Like the Grant Oneota village site described by McKusick, the Middle Missouri tradition also has its beginnings outside of the place of longest duration. Our oldest recognized sites of the tradition reveal a basic cultural assemblage and design which changed slowly over a period of perhaps 800 years and its postulated origin at the margin of the Plains contemporaneously with Oneota emergence further east is generally borne out by archaeological researches at many sites in both areas.

Recognition of a long standing rectangular-lodge agricultural tradition in the Missouri River trench upstream from the White River in South Dakota to the Knife River and beyond in North Dakota was delayed by the heavy emphasis scholars placed on the historic accounts of travelers such as Catlin and Maximilian who provided minute and detailed descriptions of the circular earthlodges in use at that time. In 1905-6 George F. Will and Herbert J. Spinden excavated a Mandan village of circular lodges (the Double Ditch site) situated a few miles upstream from Bismarck (see Will and Spinden 1906) and for 30 years thereafter, in spite of increasing evidence based on archeological surveys and accounts of native informants, students relied heavily on written documents and their interpretations to the effect that the Village tribes came onto the Missouri River

*Emeritus Professor of Anthropology, University of Idaho, Moscow, Idaho and Stanislaus State College, Turlock, California.

with circular earthlodges and had not lived there very long.

While employed by the North Dakota Historical Society to acquire archeological collections from sites near Bismarck, E. R. Steinbrueck in 1908 prepared a map of the Huff site near Mandan. He could not reconcile all surface features with circular lodges and his map of that date shows 11 large rectangular lodge outlines. Assisted by A. B. Stout, a professional surveyor, the site was remapped when Will and Spinden questioned the accuracy of the house outlines. Their map shows 12 rectangular lodges and many circular lodges. (see Wood 1967: 26). Somewhat later George F. Will mapped the site and could identify only circular lodges; in 1919 Will and Spinden again mapped the site and could see from surface features only circular lodges. (reproduced in Will 1924).

Stout and Steinbrueck (1908) also mapped the Shermer site situated opposite the Huff site on the east bank of the Missouri. This is a Mandan traditional and ceremonial village site known as *Village-Where-Turtle-Went-Back* because of an incident involving one of their turtle drums for the Okipa ceremony. Their map shows eight rectangular outlines, of which entrances are mapped for six of them (see Sperry 1968, Fig. 4). About 1916 Gilbert L. Wilson, while conducting ethnological studies at the Fort Berthold Reservation, engaged Calf Woman, who was born in the Mandan Okipa lodge at Fishhook Village, and White Calf, whose parents were the owners of the principal Lone Man bundle for the Okipa ceremony, to build a miniature ceremonial lodge. This lodge was still in Calf Woman's possession in 1929 and White Calf drew a floor plan and side view of it (Bowers 1950: 112 and 127). That year I first examined the surface outline of what the Mandans claimed was the site of an ancient lodge of Old-Woman-Who-Never-Dies. I thought it might be a natural feature as had others who had written about it. From the surface outline it was clear that if a lodge had stood there at this isolated spot it would have to be of a different design than that of a circular lodge.

Later that summer the Logan Museum of Beloit College excavated a lodge on the northern edge of the open circle believed to be the Okipa lodge at the Hensler site which had been observed by Lewis and Clark in 1804 who claimed the Mandans had lived there a decade earlier. We exposed two parallel walls of closely-spaced posts joined by a flat front facing the open circle, paired central posts and leaners set in an arch at the back of the lodge. In 1931 a large segment of a stratified site on the point where the Cheyenne River joins the Missouri broke off exposing clear evidence, even without excavating, that the lower horizon had lodges rectangular in outline, length greatly exceeding width, and that this lower horizon was entirely prehistoric. Reexamination of the Hensler lodge outline that summer confirmed our suspicions and Stout and Steinbrueck's observations that a prehistoric horizon did, in fact, underlie the period of circular lodges at least from near the mouth of the Little Missouri to the mouth of the Cheyenne.

Another link identifying the Mandans with the rectangular lodges was forged when two Mandan men, Crow's Heart and Bear-on-Flat, identified the Shermer site of rectangular lodges (see Sperry 1968) as the Mandan site of Village-Where-Turtle-Went-Back, so important in Mandan traditions. The summer had been unusually dry and little vegetation covered the site. These two men were able with ease to trace out the course they believed taken by this supernatural turtle as it walked out of the Okipa lodge to the sacred cedar and then in a direct line to the Missouri (Bowers 1950: 161 and 360).

In 1938-39 Thad C. Hecker excavated at the much-mapped Huff site for the North Dakota Historical Society, conducted extensive surveys along the banks of the Missouri and, in 1944, published with George F. Will findings which included many references to rectangular lodge sites extending nearly to the mouth of Knife River. It was no longer unpopular to cherish the belief that rectangular lodge villages were once widespread; instead many students undertook investigations to determine their distribution and relationships to historic cultures. In 1940 Elmer E. Meleen investigated the Thomas Riggs site near Pierre, a site of 22 rectangular lodges and Hurt did additional excavating there a few years later (Meleen 1949; Hurt 1953). As researches in the Missouri trough continued, it became evident that many small sites, sometimes fortified, with rectangular lodge-floor patterns of a common design within narrow limits, similar pottery types, and other cultural items were to be found in sites ranging from the Thomas Riggs site upstream to the southern edge of the Fort Berthold Reservation.

Three of us working independently set up chronologies to reflect cultural changes which we believed occurred in time. All of us are in general agreement that the small village developed into the large strongly-fortified villages of the intermediate period, these in turn to be replaced by the circular earthlodge during the late prehistoric period. All of us are in agreement that this tradition reached its highest development in the vicinity of Heart River and that this tradition in the northern area was achieved by the ancestors of the Mandans. We did, however, use slightly different terminologies to reflect cultural change in time (see Wood 1967: 144).

Pertinent to an understanding of the processes of cultural dynamics involving these first gardening-based peoples dispersed over great distances is the problem of dating the tradition. It would appear that this rapid upstream migration of gardeners was made possible because of climatically favorable conditions existing during the Neo-Atlantic interval between approximately A.D. 800-1250 and the presence in the area exploited of weakly-organized indigenous populations. Once the initial dispersal of villages over several hundred miles of the river valley was completed, subsequent reorganization into larger villages and village clusters occurred in those areas most favorable for longtime residence. From my knowledge of this valley two areas seem to have been the most favorable ones, the Big Bend area in South Dakota and the Heart River area farther upstream. In spite of the shorter growing season in the north, I would consider the Heart River region best fitted in terms of natural resources. I know the other area largely from superficial surveys and what others have written about it. A third and later concentration of villages at the mouth of Knife River was cut short prior to A.D. 1781 with the introduction of smallpox.

Of the three areas which best fitted the aboriginal needs in terms of the native cultures, I consider the region at the mouth of Heart River richest; and it was there during the 18th century that the largest native population— the Mandans—had assembled. Here the wooded bottoms were extensive, sometimes being as much as three miles or more in width; ice-dams were general during the spring thaws here due to multiple channels, adding new soils and soil moisture as well as huge piles of driftwood. On the river terraces of both banks, like a huge oval basin, the many Mandan village bands formed a nucleus to which the outlying and isolated bands were drawn. The tributary stream valleys were broad and well watered for game. The huge refuse accumulations seen there at many sites reflect long residence and it was within this restricted area, a 40-mile segment of the Missouri, that the final transition from the rectangular lodge, with its regional specialization of hide and mat covering, gave way to the circular lodge except the one used for village ceremonies. As recently as 40 years ago Mandan informants identified one of these long-occupied villages by the name of "Village of Roundlodges," implying that some villages differed from the others.

Strong (1940:380) believed that the Mobridge site (39WW-1) situated opposite the mouth of Grand River was an early Hidatsa site. In light of existing knowledge of the Hidatsa and their nearest cultural neighbors, the Mandan, this position can no longer be defended. There are no Hidatsa traditions of upstream migration along the Missouri; Crow-Hidatsa languages have few obvious cognates with the Mandan or any other Siouan language, hence they must have been long separated from such Mississippi Valley Groups as the Mandan and Chiwere-Winnebago Groups. When the Hidatsa first migrated southeastward to encounter the Mandan near the mouth of Heart River, according to traditions, they inquired where the Mandans came from and they replied "from the forks where the waters meet" and the Hidatsas said "aro'xpakua" (aro 'xpa = forks; kua = at the place of) and the Hidatsas thereafter called the Mandans *aro'xpakua*. In Lewis and Clark's time the Hidatsa were living in three earthlodge villages at the mouth of Knife River and represented the survivors of three separate and independent groups whose numbers had been sharply reduced by separation from the Crows, warfare, and the inroads of smallpox.

Of these extant groups in A.D. 1804, the Hidatsa proper and the Awaxawi claimed to have formerly lived to the northeast and east until shortly before. The Awatixa group, on the other hand, claimed long resi- dence on the Missouri upstream from the Mandan villages between Square Buttes and Knife River in a section of the valley where some sites show surface evidence of rectangular lodges. Though Hidatsa mythology and traditions make no reference to rectangular lodges, it is possible when some of these traditional Awatixa sites are excavated it will be found that at least one segment of the Crow-Hidatsa bands reached the Missouri early enough to adopt the rectangular lodge tradition from the Mandans. I know of no evidence, archeological or traditional, that any Crow-Hidatsa bands migrating overland from the east to the Missouri brought the rectangular lodge tradition with them.

By DAVIS S. BROSE*

Marshall McKusick is to be congratulated for not only the prompt report of an archaeological excavation, but the innovative concept of providing, in that publication itself, a place for commentary.

The description of the Grant Oneota Village site, and indeed the entire sequence of prehistoric habitations on the Hartley Terrace, is clear and succinct. Indeed, it is with rare honesty that McKusick describes the problems involved in locating settlement data on a sun-baked, machine-crossed excavation unit. McKusick is also scrupulously honest in distinguishing his interpretations from the data presented. The profession could stand more of this.

Among at least four archaeological sites on a terrace adjacent to the Upper, or Little Iowa River, McKusick describes his excavations at the Grant Village, an early Oneota site overlying what appeared to be the early Effigy Mound Lane Group. The Grant Village site appears to have been a small summer village occupied during the eleventh century A.D. McKusick has uncovered a series of post molds indicating, clearly, a new type of structure for Oneota sites reported in Iowa. These consist of at least four longhouses, offering some evidence to counter a number of earlier hypotheses regarding the development of Oneota out of a Middle Mississippian base. The post mold patterns indicate some period of occupation, with overlapping and rebuilt lines, so that it is unclear exactly how much of the site may have been occupied at any one time. Some evaluation of this possibility must be included before demographic parameters are estimated.

In this respect an analysis of post mold diameters is of questionable value. Recent studies (Brose 1970) have indicated that some amount of the diameter represents organic staining beyond the actual limits of the post itself. In the light sandy soils of the upper Great Lakes this can amount to a factor of as much as 35 percent within a period of less than 1,000 years. Depending on soil porosity and precipitation patterns, variations in post mold diameters may not reflect cultural choice on the part of those who erected the structures represented.

*Associate Professor of Anthropology, Case Western Reserve University, Cleveland, Ohio.

This becomes important especially when one attempts to estimate the methods of construction involved in such houses. Small diameter saplings may have been flexible enough to tie together without multiple sections.

McKusick is also to be complimented in his very full ethnographic description of house types and house constructions. He has taken great pains to indicate the amount of variation, seasonal (and functional?) that existed in the prairie area. While McKusick has offered five different reasons to account for this diversity, at least among the Winnebago, it would seem that in terms of cultural evolution many of these are subsumed under the selective pressures which would have operated to require special types of structures for different seasonal activities. Indeed similar seasonal variations in structures were reported for the Huron by Brébeuf in 1636 (Thwaites 1901). McKusick's reconstructions of the Grant Village houses seem quite reasonable. It is interesting to note that raccoon *baculae* were recovered from storage pits within the village: as McKusick has reported, among the Potawatomi such bones were used as mat sewing awls and needles (p. 36).

In terms of the major site settlement plan McKusick has been quite careful in his insistence on divorcing the data from his speculations. The one place where this does not seem to have occurred is in the projection of a fourth house to complete the symmetry of the site. Indeed there is a temporal problem involved in the nature of these occupations. There do seem to be questions in terms of the location of certain pre-Grant Village mounds. There has been considerable rebuilding (indicating reoccupation of unknown duration) at the village site itself. Surely all of these render the demographic reconstructions questionable. Still, the game is worth the candle. In this respect one would like to know whether the present north village boundary, i.e., the Terrace crest, is a relatively recent erosional phenomenon.

McKusick rightly stresses the fact that the use of faunal analyses for population reconstructions is unacceptable. This has been brought into considerable relief by John Guilday in his faunal analysis of the Fort Ligonier, Pennsylvania materials. Guilday recovered enough faunal remains to have provided meat for one man for 100 days, or 100 men for one day, in spite of the fact that the historical records unambiguously state that at least 150 men occupied the site for nearly three years.

The estimations of population then can only come from the settlement pattern analysis: here indeed we must assume that the houses are contemporaneously occupied. Following this, McKusick's reconstruction of ten to twelve nuclear families per house for a total summer village population of 200 people seems quite reasonable. McKusick's suggestions on the stability of width (probably a factor of sapling diameter and flexibility as well as the type of wood involved in the construction [Brose 1970]) as opposed to variations in length representing the extent of residential kin groups is certainly worth further exploration: in this respect some estimation of strength of lineage affiliation and trends in lineage affiliation might be generated by a chronologically ordered number of longhouse modules ("12-foot sections"). A goodness of fit test between the order of site houses by number of modules per structure and the chronological order independently determined should demonstrate the existence of kinship trends. Similarly a measure of coefficient of variation within village for modular number of structures might indicate whether lineage extensions fluctuate as the result of other socio-cultural or ecological parameters. These could be tied into a ceramic attribute analysis such as initiated by James Deetz (1965) in a study of the Medicine Creek Arikara materials. Unfortunately the present report gives no indication of ceramic attribute associations and therefore cannot be used in this way.

In terms of the description of the artifacts, the report is somewhat disappointing. While punctate size appears to be a major criterion of ceramic decoration we have neither the mean nor standard deviation for punctate size. In addition, although a plate of rim profiles is given, there is no frequency for any particular rim profile occurrence. Furthermore it is virtually impossible to reconstruct the vessel morphology and decoration from the descriptions presented. While "The Grant Type" is vaguely described, variations from this modal ceramic concatenation are impossible to determine from the data presented.

In terms of his discussion of lithic materials McKusick also has neglected to provide what I would consider basic descriptive statistics so that some estimation of variability within populations can be obtained. Here perhaps the fault is not primarily McKusick's as he was working with a rather limited sample. Eventually someone will have to go back and redo the lithic technology of most of the Iowa Oneota sites. As McKusick has indicated this will not be easy for most of the early collections were highly biased. This can be demonstrated by taking his Table 7 and confirming his suspicions that there has been a great deal of selectivity for projectile points. If the Allamakee County sites were initially similar in lithic frequencies (by flaked stone type groups) to the Grant Village site, the methods of sampling have rendered earlier collections virtually useless for comparative purposes.

With these latter exceptions McKusick's report is excellent, especially his concern with deriving ethnographic analogs to explain the archaeological variability recovered.

CHIPPED STONE GROUP FREQUENCIES FROM McKUSICK (1972)
    TABLE 7

	Projectile Points	Bifacial Knives	Unifacial Scrapers	Pointed Drills	TOTAL
ALLAMAKEE SITES	102	40	79	4	225
GRANT VILLAGE	13	24	42	7	86
TOTAL					311

Chi Square = 28.5977
d.f.   = 3
p   = .001

By HESTER A. DAVIS*

The description of Quapaw houses from Joutel's account has been quoted on pages 24-25, and problems of archaeological correlations in Arkansas are summarized on pages 59-60. I feel completely inadequate to comment on any possible relationships with Oneota because I have not as yet done the necessary study of the literature. In addition, I believe the archaeological evidence on the Quapaw to be too inadequate—either concerning long-houses or anything else—at the moment, to warrant any conclusions concerning relationships with other areas.

The illustration in McGimsey (1969) of the Quapaw house is an "artist's reconstruction" from Joutel's description. He says they were long (in relation to what?), and bark covered. As mentioned on pages 59-60, Ford found a rectangular house at Menard, but no evidence of bark, and in fact in other areas of probable houses found abundant evidence of wattle and daub. Burney McClurkan, of the Arkansas Archeological Survey, has been testing a reputed Quapaw site (Moore Bayou site) this spring, in the surface collection from which were willow leaf points and Wallace Incised sherds. The house pattern

*State Archeologist, Arkansas Archeological Survey, University of Arkansas Museum, Fayetteville, Arkansas.

he found was a typical, wall-trench, square Mississippian house. In other words, in terms of longhouses in the Quapaw occupation, the archaeological evidence simply isn't there yet. Rectangular houses, yes, quite possibly, but *long* rectangular houses, no. I'm inclined to be cautious.

By HENRY P. FIELD*

In regard to post holes on a village site: I am sure we saw many of them on the nearby Flatiron Terrace, upstream from the Grant site, and we did not recognize them for what they were. The reason we did *not* recognize them was that the site was demolished by the gravel moving machinery cutting into it by vertical slicing as one would cut up a loaf of bread, so we always saw only the *profile* and not the surface uncovered as cleanly as you did at the Grant site. Stripping was roughly done.

The gravel removal went on more or less continuously for a good many years. Most of our observations and activities took place during the late 1930s and the early 1940s. The site is completely destroyed now—leveled and gone. My field notes from this period are now on file in your office, and I call your attention to the description on page two of these notes which reads: "Apparently a distinction must be made between some pits which were firepits, where beds of coals had been produced many times by building good-sized fires, and refuse pits in which mere garbage and refuse had been dumped to get rid of it. Some pits may have served both purposes, first being used for barbecuing large animals and preparing food, and then, later, being filled in with refuse and dirt. The narrow 'wedge-shaped' pits seem to have been post holes refilled with topsoil." The enclosed picture (figure 55 upper) shows the Flatiron Terrace cut by the gravel machinery, and the pits and refilled post holes can be seen.

---

*Former member of Ellison Orr's field crew, and currently a dentist in Decorah, Iowa.

By ELIZABETH J. GLENN*

Dr. McKusick has two stated objectives in the presentation of his Grant site data: one objective is a discussion of house types in association with early Oneota materials at the Grant village; and, the other, the development of the possibility of a cultural *group continuity* for Oneota in that all-important region of the Upper Iowa River. Implications arising from his discussion of this site bear on Oneota origins, taxonomy, and cultural associations. As a physical anthropologist, it would be difficult for me to comment too extensively on the cultural material and its associations. However, I might, on the basis of a recent comparative study of Oneota skeletal series (Glenn 1971MS) add comments on some of the implications Dr. McKusick has raised about Oneota origins and inter-relationships.

The discovery of a village with distinct residence patterns associated with Oneota is a notable contribution in this pottery-defined archaeological complex. From his excavation data, the author develops very thoroughly and realistically the implications of the house forms within the context of the Grant site itself. The supportive evidence, ethnographic and ethnohistoric, gives ample background for his final descriptive framework. Most significant is the association of a longhouse-style residence with very early, but developed, Oneota rather than the diagnostic Middle Mississippian structure predicted by Griffin in 1960.

The fact that Griffin's speculation (1960) that Middle Mississippian house types would be found in association with early Oneota materials should be demonstrated to be partially incorrect is hardly surprising. Since his hypothesis was based on the assumption of Middle Mississippian derivation for Oneota, and since most recent information indicates that this is not the case, it would seem that Griffin's assumption could be disposed of with the rest of the theory. A multivariate discriminant analysis of Oneota skeletal material is also supportive of this stance.

Some of the results of this analysis are given in figures 56 and 57. Both of these figures represent the distributions of individuals and/or groups in discriminant space. Both are two dimensional in that they are based on discriminant functions 1 (x) and 2 (y)—the functions which in combination account for 75 percent or more of the total variability in the comparisons discussed here.

In figure 56, 113 Oneota crania, grouped according to their archaeological associations, were compared to archaeological populations delineated by George K. Neumann as being types representative of the physical diversification in the area of Oneota distribution. The type population of particular concern here is

---

*Assistant Professor of Anthropology, Ball State University, Muncie, Indiana.

the Muskogid composed of 54 adult male crania found in association with Middle Mississippian components in Illinois. To roughly ascertain how closely Oneota populations "resemble" people associated with Middle Mississippian cultures, one would be interested in the amount of overlap between these population distributions represented in figure 56 by encirclement.

In figure 56, the only Oneota population showing a distinct overlap with the Muskogid series was a very small sample (3 crania) from the Bryan site in Minnesota. Although the physical relationship is unquestionable, the explanation for this occurrence need not include a Middle Mississippian derivation for this early Oneota manifestation. Indeed, considering the small sample size and considering recent evidence pertaining to Oneota-Middle Mississippian relationships, one would tend to de-accentuate this possibility. Furthermore, the lack of relationship of all other Oneota populations to the Middle Mississippian would further substantiate theories negating a derivational affiliation between these traditions.

Another analysis was made using only the Oneota and Oneota-associated cranial material to demonstrate some of the relationships within the tradition. The results of this analysis are found in figure 57 where the function 1 and 2 values are given individually by letter and group clusters are encircled.

As can be seen in figure 57, there seems to be a physical "group continuity" between the Wisconsin Grand River and Lake Winnebago populations which does not exist between Grand River and the trans-Mississippi (Orr and Peripheral) Oneota. Nor does there seem to be as strong a relationship between the Wisconsin and trans-Mississippi Oneota peoples as there is between the various trans-Mississippi Oneota populations. This relative discontinuity between the statistical distributions of the Wisconsin and trans-Mississippi Oneota populations is a further substantiation of linguistic, archaeological, and traditional evidences of separation between these peoples.

When the combined series of Correctionville-Blue Earth, Leary, Blood Run, and Utz (Peripheral Oneota) is compared to the series from various components of Minnesota and Upper Iowa River Orr, there is found to be very little differentiation between them (figure 57). This is not to say the total trans-Mississippi population is homogeneous, but rather, that individuals from all these sites fall within the same distribution range with no particular archaeological group forming its own cluster. The lack of population differentiation in trans-Mississippi Oneota would tend to support a broader taxonomy of these Oneota cultural manifestations. At least it may indicate that the populations of various *group continuities* described in this publication and in Henning (1970) were not living in a situation of complete isolation from one another for a long period of time. This would seem to reinforce Henning's interpretation of the melting pot nature of at least the Grand River Missouri *group continuity* and his inclusive taxonomic construct of the Orr Phase (1970).

To summarize the physical relationships demonstrated by these analyses, one can state that they show: a lack of affiliation between Oneota and Middle Mississippian populations; a discontinuity between Wisconsin and trans-Mississippi Oneota peoples; and a lack of differentiation between the crania found in various Oneota sites west of the Mississippi. The latter relationship seems to be the only one in conflict with McKusick's conclusions. If one were to assume that pottery differences could be a more sensitive evaluative category than population differences for an understanding of the relationships between what must have been non-isolated, localized continuities, the more specific taxonomic breakdown preferred by McKusick might better benefit that understanding. Unfortunately, the lack of extensive comparative data in this publication makes it difficult for one not working directly with Oneota archaeological materials to evaluate this problem relative to the Grant site and its localized continuity.

By DALE R. HENNING*

The Grant Oneota site report is not, in my estimation, ready for publication. It is obviously the result of unbridled enthusiasm coupled with too little time for thorough and considered effort. Occasionally, a site excavation is technically good, but the quality of the final report is substandard due to pressures upon the author from teaching and other research. I wish most sincerely that this were true of the Grant Oneota research project; judging from this report, the whole effort, from the removal of the first spadeful of soil to the final period, appears to have been poorly planned and badly executed. The basic problem appears to have been one of unconscionable haste from beginning to end.

Modern excavation techniques do not involve the use of shovel and bull-dozer to clear large areas (5-8,000 square feet) unless 1) the site is immediately threatened by inundation, total removal or construction, 2) the overburden being removed contains *no* evidence of occupation, or 3) the occupational evidence is so well known that its retention serves no purpose pertinent to the problems being attacked. I have made a number of surface collections from the surface of the Hartley Terrace; it was on the portion of the terrace identified by McKusick as the Grant site that village debris was encountered in greatest quantities. Materials recovered in my collections were deposited with the State Archaeologist at The University of Iowa Archaeological Laboratory, Iowa City, under the site number 13 AM 53. Therefore, I was surprised to learn that "...the site was discovered by accident, previous investigators on the terrace having no knowledge of its existence..." (p. 13). Judging from the quantities of material recovered from

---

*Associate Professor of Anthropology, University of Nebraska, Lincoln, Nebraska.

the surface of the Grant site in the past, I find it difficult to believe that there was no surface evidence and that materials in the plow zone were so scarce as to warrant shoveling or bulldozing aside the entire deposit above the "unmixed loess" (p. 13). The site was *not* being salvaged from immediate destruction, there was *some* village debris in the plow zone and even though it is characterized as "sparse" (p. 13) and perhaps partially mixed by plowing, it was data vital to our proper understanding of Grant occupation patterns. I am certain that a great deal of important information was tossed aside in an effort to "get at" as many house outlines as possible in a six-week period.

Was this immense effort, involving over thirty excavators and a bulldozer, plus emergency funding provided by the State Executive Council (p. 12) really worthwhile? What do we have to work with after this hasty, immense expenditure of money, machinery and manpower? We have house outlines from perhaps eight structures, materials from 43 storage pits or hearths, nearly 1,200 potsherds, chipped and pecked and ground stone tools, bone objects and a few other items, some of which will be discussed below. These bits of hard data coupled with three radiocarbon dates are intriguing but not sufficiently revealing.

The site was important; we needed every scrap of information available from it. The Grant site was not excavated with maximal recovery in mind. A far better plan of recovery would have involved considerably less digging per season; the excavations would have employed more intensive techniques of recovery throughout the site amounting to equal house outline data coupled with recovery of data vital to the aims of modern archaeology. Intensive recovery would minimally involve ¼" screening of *all* soil above the "unmixed loess" (after all, the materials above the "unmixed loess" constituted all evidence for house occupations). Further, portions of the house fill, whether plow zone or immediately beneath it, should have been subjected to hydraulic screening through 1/8" mesh. All pit and hearth fill should have been subjected to 1/8" hydraulic screening and flotation. The water screening of all soil from *one* (p. 13) of 43 features is statistically unsound, at best. The excavation program which Dr. McKusick elected to complete in six weeks should have taken at least five eight-week summer seasons, utilizing currently acceptable procedures. The rewards for proceeding slowly and methodically would have been more than worthwhile if only in terms of understanding the subsistence system. What, then, was the rationale for haste at the Grant site? The location of house outlines no longer constitutes a problem of good anthropological archaeology and has not for several decades.

Haste and carelessness also characterize the descriptive portions. There are no inventories of materials other than bodysherds, rimsherds and "total artifacts" from the nearly 43 pits and hearths excavated. The reader is not offered the data in a format suitable for reinterpretation, should he desire. Given 43 features in a site, might one not conclude that they should yield information pertinent to house "use-area," tool manufacture and function, food processing, even social organization? None of this kind of information can be abstracted using the Grant site report.

In Chapter 6, McKusick has broken with "standard" procedures of artifact descriptions, offering as inclusive categories Shaped Stone, Other Materials, Flaked Stone, and Pottery. Under Shaped Stone, we find Abrading tools, Grinding artifacts, Hammering tools, Pipes and tablets, and Miscellaneous. The problems confronting the reader of this chapter are numerous. A few examples follow. On page 46, under "Hammering tools," there is one tool described. That tool is identified as a celt, but "the usage marks are suggestive of a chisel function for this celt" (p. 46). There are significant functional differences between "hammering tools," "celts" and "chisels." What does McKusick think this item is? Under Pipes and tablets, we are offered the fact that both are "extremely rare" (p. 46) and, indeed they are. There are no pipes discussed from Grant at all; there is one small tablet with a V-shaped decoration which "resembles the so-called 'turkey track' petroglyph." Generally, the latter is characterized by three toes forward and one back. Under Other Materials (p. 47), a "bison scapula hoe" is identified. The scapular blade is missing which technically renders it identifiable only as a "modified bison scapula"; it might as well have been identified as a "sickle." Also included in this category is a "copper ornament" "...made from a rolled sheet" (p.47). By searching the captions (separated from the illustrations they describe) one finds that the copper ornament is tubular (p.88). Why not describe it as a rolled tubular copper bead? The Flaked Stone and Pottery categories are similarly described; comparison with other Oneota site materials is difficult at best.

The photographs are clear and clean; they are potentially useful. But, why did the editor omit the letter designations on plates which are referred to throughout the text and under the list of Illustrations? The reader must take the items in some sort of assumed logical order or guess which item is being referred to.

The Grant site was important to the growing body of information pertinent to Oneota origins and the evolution of Oneota culture. With this topic in mind, I am surprised at McKusick's interpretation of the meaning of his three radiocarbon dates. If they do indeed date Oneota occupations on the Grant site (remember, Grant is a two-component site with two Woodland mounds included within its parameters), they offer a range of time from about A.D. 900 to nearly 1300. McKusick, following Hall (1962) and Baerreis and Bryson (1965) states that "...by A.D. 1000 Oneota culture had already separated from its Middle Mississippian forebearers (sic)" (p.1). Judging from his discussion of the Wisconsin sites (p. 54-57), McKusick agrees that the Oneota ceramic tradition was in existence by A.D. 1000, but *still* sees it as derived from a Middle Mississippian base (p. 1, p. 64). Careful attention to the paper by Hall (1966), which is referred to in the bibliography, should have revealed the fact that the Grant site may have been occupied at a time *antecedent to* the development of the Early Old Village Phase at Cahokia (Hall 1965:8). Here is potentially good evidence for an independent development of Oneota culture simultaneous to, but with little influence from, the evolving Mississippian tradition at Cahokia. This is a point which I have emphasized (Henning 1970), but McKusick has again either failed to notice or has chosen to ignore.

The monograph is not prepared for publication. To properly review it would involve a complete re-analysis of each hypothesis, the rewriting of the descriptive passages and the redigging of the site. Not all these endeavors are possible (the site cannot be re-excavated); there is not time for those options remaining. The author should rewrite and the editor should edit.

By WILLIAM M. HURLEY*

The Grant Oneota Village by Marshall McKusick represents a very informative report dealing with a complex, multi-component, restricted area on the Upper Iowa River. The Iowa components confined to the Hartley Terrace appear to represent occupations from *circa* A.D. 870 to 1740, which are ordered according to two Late Woodland components and two Oneota Orr Focus components. Perhaps the presence of these occupations in a horizontally and vertically confined area raises some questions concerning artifact separation; however, McKusick appears to have the provenience factors well under control. McKusick introduces various hypotheses by Baerreis and Bryson, and Griffin, for the origin, expansion and decline of Oneota. The believed "cultural adaptation" to the Oneota tradition (after Hall?), together with the evidence for Oneota in northeast Iowa as seen from various archaeological reports, leaves McKusick somewhat unhappy with the systems utilized to describe Oneota and the Orr Focus (McKusick, Wedel, Hall, Henning, and Straffin). He offers his own four-fold terminology which still needs to be supported by further data from other sites in the area.

The main discussion of the excavations centers on the Grant Village with comparative ethnographic and ethnohistoric data introduced after the radiocarbon determinations are reported for the Hartley Terrace sites. The dates and number and types of houses present at the Orr Focus Grant Village are a surprise as Orr Focus houses had not been reported for Iowa. The dates indicate that the ordering of Oneota into various sequential foci is not the simple concept of focus

*Associate Professor of Anthropology, University of Toronto, Toronto, Canada.

replacement through time *e.g.* Grand River/Nashonomy—Lake Winnebago—Orr foci (i.e. Gibbon 1972), but that each of the foci may have had a long and involved chronological history (after Hall's chronological chart, 1962) which can only be ascertained by more site excavations. In Wisconsin the number of well-excavated and reported Oneota sites number less than six. At the present time the house sizes seem quite large for so early a site, but maybe the early dates once rejected by David Gradwohl for Oneota in the Des Moines Valley may now be more acceptable. Work presently (June 1972) being conducted by a crew from the University of Toronto at a prehistoric Orr Focus site near Pepin, Wisconsin (47PE-7 and 47PE-12) which has a village area of 11 1/2 acres indicates that one fully-exposed house is only 10 by 20 feet, and semi-subterranean without external support posts. I am using this report in the field as an on-the-site guide to Oneota research, and the quickness of publishing this report is to be commended.

It would seem that more work should be done at the Grant Village to explore further houses and to increase the artifact yield. This report indicates that the lively subject of the when, how and why of Oneota will be continued for many years in a healthy scientific series of reports, "facts" and hypotheses.

By FLOYD G. LOUNSBURY*

I am very much interested in the Iroquois parallels. I have gone through the report with this in mind, and have paid special attention to the section of Conclusions, but I'm not enough of an expert on things other than language to be able to say anything enlightening. I have puzzled over the name *Oneota* in the past. It does "look" Iroquoian. Yet it cannot be pinned down, and I can do no better than McKusick has done (page 4), following M. Wedel (1959:6-7). All I can say is that the visiting Oneidas must have completely misunderstood McGee's question, for they appear to have given him their name for themselves rather than a name for the Upper Iowa River. Their name for their own tribal and linguistic identity is *Onʌ̃yoteʔ*, in which *o*- is a third person generic or neuter-objective pronominal prefix, -nʌ̃y-is the incorporated noun root for "stone," -*ot*- is a verb root for "to set, or be set (depending on inflection) in an upright position," and -*eʔ* is perfective aspect suffix making this a perfect-passive participial form. It is commonly translated "Standing Stone." As for other possible Iroquois antecedents for the name *Oneota*, I can think of none. I have looked through my lexical files and also Chafe's Seneca dictionary, and I see no reasonable possibilities that could have anything to do with a river.

---

*Professor of Anthropology, Yale University, New Haven, Connecticut.

By G. RICHARD PESKE*

The Grant Village site report adds critical new data to Oneota studies and at the same time forces Oneota prehistorians into reformulating questions about this major cultural phase in the Midwest. The major new data pertain to settlement pattern (i.e., longhouses and their relationship in a village setting) and early Oneota origins (i.e., temporal placement in the 11th century A.D.).

Some archeologists may quibble over the definition of "longhouse" by taking the League of the Iroquois houses as a model for their definition. In this case, the "longhouses" of Grant Village differ in their structure from those of the Iroquois; notably in the absence of structural features reflecting family compartments, benches, a linear series of hearths, and having rounded rather than square ends. Regardless of definitional qualms, the Grant Village "longhouses" are large structures which are best interpreted, due to their number and internal features, as dwellings rather than ceremonial structures which are ethnographically known from Central Algonkian groups. Furthermore, their size is indicative of a residential unit which houses more than one nuclear family. The presence of these multifamily dwellings at a number of Oneota sites is suggestive of either a tribal level of socio-political integration with a clan kinship base or the beginnings of social ranking. Along this line, Guy Gibbon (1969MS;1972) has suggested that the origins of Oneota in Wisconsin coincide with a shift from a band to a tribal level of socio-political integration. This proposed shift would probably also be explainable in terms of a new agricultural technology and emphasis which originates and spreads concomitantly with early Mississippian culture, including Oneota from about A.D. 800-1100. Gibbon (*Ibid.*) also reports long oval houses from the Walker-Hooper and Bornick sites, which are Grand River Focus dating to the 12th century A.D. These houses are not as long or as wide as those at Grant Village.

I view multifamily dwellings in the Midwest including the houses at Grant Village as an indicator of a tribal or simple ranking social organization which has an appreciable maize agriculture subsistance base. However, we must also contend with single nuclear family dwellings which are associated with contemporary Middle Mississippian sites across the Mississippi drainage including Cahokia and Aztalan. These dwellings, in a Middle Mississippian setting, may reflect a higher level of socio-political integration of a chiefdom or state.

The houses from Carcajou Point described by Hall (1962), and those I excavated but have not yet published, are of the general rectangular type with wall trench construction which is a major type at both Cahokia and Aztalan. In addition to these houses, in my excavations at Carcajou Point, I encountered

*Instructor of Anthropology, University of Wisconsin, Milwaukee, Wisconsin.

a palisade segment of large post molds and deep wall trench construction which is similar to the palisade construction at Cahokia and Aztalan.

The question arises as to whether or not Carcajou Point is more similar to a Middle Mississippian adaptation than to Oneota? Perhaps the stress on ceramic relationships between sites has obfuscated studies of cultural adaptation. In reference to the Hartley Terrace sites, a comparison of Grant Village, Lane Enclosure, and Hartley Fort sites on a basis of settlement pattern, ecology, and subsistance would elucidate problems of cultural adaptational changes in terms of Late Woodland and Oneota.

The Grant Village site is early in the Oneota sequence which is borne out both by radiocarbon dates and ceramic analyses. The addition of this site to the roster of early Oneota sites supports a date of Oneota origin which is contemporaneous with early Middle Mississippian development at about A.D. 900-1000. Certainly Middle Mississippi and Oneota development are related but I view them as concomitant and both heavily influenced by new kinds of agriculture.

In terms of the Grant Village–Lane Enclosure ceramic comparisons, Grant Village is seriated as predating the Lane Enclosure site. A number of attribute differences are meaningful as a broad time horizon marker across the Upper Mississippi Valley and into Eastern Wisconsin. These include: 1) the earlier prevalence of medium trailing in deference to later narrow trailing, 2) the early dominance of low rims to the later higher rim preference, and 3) the early use of punctates as border elements in contrast to the later use of punctate fillers within an enclosed area. In addition to ceramics as a time marker, in Wisconsin and perhaps also in Iowa, catlinite is absent or extremely rare in Oneota components until about A.D. 1100-1200.

The use of shell leaching in ceramics as a relative dating technique is poor as is attested to by differential leaching within a site component. At Lasley's Point in Wisconsin, sherds which were in dense deposits (e.g., midden heaps) or with mollusc shell refuse, had very little leaching but sherds found off of the dense deposits would be leached. Time is only one factor in the leaching process; there are many other factors which affect the leaching process and I would not accept the relative dating between Lane Enclosure and Grant Village on this basis.

In terms of settlement type, a "longhouse" does not necessarily mean a summer dwelling only. More data is needed for analyses of prehistoric fauna and flora in relationship to seasonal site usage. A model of seasonal rounds also should be developed for application to portions of a village population rather than to the whole village. Frequently in the Great Lakes, a portion of the local society would leave the village to exploit seasonal resources but the village itself would not be totally abandoned.

More house type and settlement pattern data are needed to answer many questions pertaining to Oneota. In this regard, a critical prehistoric cultural division of Oneota is the Lake Winnebago Focus. Although the present data

(Peske 1966) suggest a complex settlement pattern including extensive agricultural fields, no houses have been excavated. This is unfortunate because the greatest numbers of kinds of houses including gabled houses have been mentioned in Winnebago ethnography (Radin 1923).

The Grant Village site is an important contribution to Oneota research and like many contributions it forces a new set of questions into this research.

AUTHOR'S REPLY

The format of *Current Anthropology* provides a lengthy article over a controversial subject, printed together with comments by specialists who may have other views to express, and answered in an author's reply. This has proven to be a highly invigorating approach to academic questions, and one could wish that the *American Anthropologist* and *American Antiquity* would occasionally print articles in this style. As mentioned by Brose this format has not been previously applied to monograph length studies. I thought it would be a useful experiment because Oneota studies are incomplete, much information is unpublished, and opinions differ on taxonomy, origins, relationships, and settlement patterns.

There are practical problems stemming from the use of this format which include delays and considerable added expense, and I would not indiscriminantly urge that this approach be adopted by the profession. Selective use, where subject matter warrants, will repay the inconvenience. By the time this monograph is finally ready for distribution, it will have been *in press* fourteen months. There was a delay in plate and photo-offset production which set back the time schedule for circulating advance copies, and this was followed by the problems of extending contributors' due dates and my own, which are familiar to every editor. If this had not been done, too few comments would have been received to justify holding the monograph open. The production was further plagued with proof errors in the advance copies necessitating a complete re-run. The publication date and Library of Congress number were assigned as of 1971, and the finally issued report emerged in late 1973, a situation not calculated to improve the temper of printers. These delays could have been less, and the discussion by specialists and additional information undoubtedly makes up for the inconvenience.

In reviewing the comments, I find great difficulty discussing the remarks by Dale Henning, for he has neither discussed the conclusions, nor added new information. I was curious as to how he regarded the conceptual taxonomic problem of transforming the Midwestern Taxonomic Method foci into diachronic phases, such as his Orr Phase, and whether he still considered the Blue Island culture of eastern Illinois to be part of it. There were a number of other points which would have been a contribution and could be discussed without rancor, but he has chosen different grounds. When he says this publication is "hasty," and "ill-conceived," one must in fairness to him mention that the advance copies averaged four or five typographic errors for each sixteen page signature, and fourteen specimen figures lacked the identifying letters listed in the discussion of illustrations. As mentioned, these corrections were made prior to publication. There is even less excuse for his other remarks.

Was the Grant Site Previously Known? Henning says it was a site profusely strewn with artifacts, and previously recorded by him under the site designation 13AM-57. The facts of the matter are as follows. Colonel Norris recorded a number of sites on this terrace in 1882 but neither his site plan (reproduced as figure 2) nor his summary of excavations published by Thomas (1894) makes any reference to a village in the area of the Grant village, although he located a number of other sites including some which cannot be found today (see my discussion pages 7-8). About the turn of the century, and thereafter at intervals, Ellison Orr revisited the Hartley Terrace on a number of occasions. Although an amateur, he was finally employed as field supervisor of the now long-defunct Iowa Archaeological Survey under Charles R. Keyes. Ellison Orr *spent weeks on the Hartley Terrace during 1934 and 1936* digging the Lane Mounds, including mounds which lie at the periphery of the Grant village. There are detailed manuscript reports of his activity (Orr 1948MS, 1963: various volumes) but nowhere in his reports does he identify the village site in the mound group he was excavating. I later reviewed the terrace sites (McKusick 1964a) but did not recognize the Grant village from surface evidence, and found it by accident in 1970 when a few Oneota sherds began to appear in our trenches as has been explained. Henning now says this site 13AM-57 is the Grant village. We have Henning's site sheet on file. The collection was made in 1950 and the site sheet is dated 1959 both prior to my arrival at The University of Iowa. The site sheet has no description of the site whatever, no site name, no identification of it as Oneota, and no sketch map of its location. The only information is the quadrant location. His coordinates read that it was in the NE quarter of the SW quarter of Section 36, Range 5W, Township 100N. The Hartley Terrace plan (figure 1, page 90) shows these coordinates place 13AM-57 somewhere in the vicinity of the Lane Enclosure, rather than at the Grant village. A quarter section is a very large square tract half a mile to a side. Thus, when Henning located 13AM-57 in the *southwest quarter section* and the Grant village site is located in the *southeast quarter section,* this becomes a gross difference or misidentification. I should like to think his error was due to his transposition of letters, if indeed we are talking about the Grant village (13AM-201) and Henning's unnamed site (13AM-57) being one-and-the-same. However, the coordinate system locates sites within the nearest quarter of the quarter section, or sixteenth section, a quarter mile on each side of the square. It makes a great deal of difference where this quarter mile square area containing a site is situated. Let us assume as a case in point that Henning somehow hastily jotted down the notation NE quarter of the SW quarter, when in fact he meant the NE quarter of the SE quarter. Could this have been possible? I don't think so because if you review this transposed location on the plan (figure 1) you arrive at a site location entirely off the terrace, down on the mud flats, somewhere in the three-quarters-of-a-mile-line between the Hartley Terrace and the Upper Iowa River. But let us assume that Henning accidentally transposed his designation writing NE of SW, but intending

NW of SW, when in fact the Grant village is NW of NE. The NW of SW transposition assumption does not work out very well because this would put Henning's 13AM-57 off the terrace, out on the flood plain, and on the wrong side of the river. As I have shown, if you assume that either of Henning's quadrant designations is correct and the other was transposed, you will be entirely off the terrace. A third transposition is possible; that Henning somehow carelessly reversed quarter and sixteenth sections, writing NE of SW when he meant SW of NE. This is not very helpful, for this would again put his site location somewhere in the mud flats. I don't know how to account for all of this.

Henning collected from the surface of 13AM-57, and although no site sheet information is present, a note on his specimens shows they were picked up on two different days in 1950. He now recalls, more than two decades later, that the location *had the greatest concentration of artifacts on the Hartley Terrace.* This is astonishing news indeed, for no previous investigator reported this rich area, neither Norris, Orr, nor McKusick. And I may add that Henning (1961) published a descriptive study of pottery he dug out somewhere from the Lane Enclosure. He has no statement about where the pottery came from within the Lane Enclosure, provides no site map or description, and no provenience information is with the collection itself in the Archaeological Laboratory. The reason I mention this is that in the 1961 published version of his 1959 master's thesis written at The University of Iowa under Reynold Ruppe, Henning describes the Oneota pottery of the Hartley Terrace from his diggings at the Lane Enclosure, but he makes no mention that the richest concentration of artifacts is elsewhere. In point of fact he makes no mention of 13AM-57 whatever, wherever it may lie. The collection of artifacts Henning obtained from 13AM-57, on two different days is in the Archaeological Laboratory, Accession 70. This collection *in total* contains 45 artifacts and pieces of flaking waste, but *not a single scrap of pottery.* The artifacts include two shell beads, a very small, fragmentary catlinite pendant, three fragmentary triangular arrowheads, and the remainder are incomplete fragments of flaked unifacial and bifacial tools. I see no reason why this assemblage could not be Oneota, although we found comparable projectile points at the Late Woodland Hartley Fort on the terrace. The catlinite pendant fragment is a surprise to me, if it is indeed associated with the Grant Village, because I suspect that catlinite is extremely rare or absent in early Oneota sites in this area, and none occurred in the fill of the 40 Grant site storage pits screened through quarter-inch mesh. Peske raises the same point about the rarity or absence of catlinite at early Oneota sites in Wisconsin (see page 165).

The Hartley Terrace is in the soil bank and thickly planted grass now makes it impossible to surface collect. However, the Lane Enclosure storage pits were the most solidly packed with huge sherds and other debris of any comparable features I have seen in the midwest. By way of contrast the Grant Village storage pits were among the sparsest. The very small sherd samples were not due to any grossness in excavation technique, for we used quarter-inch screens. The sherds were simply not there in quantity. As the summary totals show (table 1, page 76), 50 to 77 percent of all classes of finds came from delineated storage pits, and in my earlier description I noted (page 13) that the rare sherds and chipping waste occurred for the most part with underlying storage pits, but above the level where pit outlines could be defined.

All of this leads me to conclude that Henning's observations in 1950 may originally have coincided with those of Orr and myself. Orr, working at the Lane Mounds during parts of two summers, had to walk over the Grant village twice every day because of the position of the private access dirt road leading up from the Lane farm, a road which had no alternative location to the terrace. He worked at mounds adjacent to the village site. I suspect he and his crew probably ate their lunches under the same huge tree that we did, because there are very limited possibilities on that part of the terrace; and if this is correct, he had to recross the Grant Village another two times each day. At no time did he recognize the village from surface remains. Henning seems to have noticed chipping waste and artifacts reportedly from this area, but he did not collect a single potsherd. I found potsherds to be extremely sparse in the excavations. To this extent we are all in agreement. But now Henning is shifting his views, saying this area is the richest artifact area on the terrace, and it seems to me his purpose in alleging this is to make me out to be some sort of monster destroyer of valuable antiquities.

I am vacating 13AM-57 as a site designation because there is a gross discrepancy in Henning's 1959 and 1972 coordinate locations, and no corroborating description appears. The official state record now reads, "13AM-57 vacated for reassignment because of inconsistency in location. Originally attributed to an area near the Lane Enclosure (13AM-200), it was subsequently attributed to the Grant Village (13AM-201). Accession 70 with 13AM-57 without pottery attributed to Oneota." The vacating report then cites the discussion from this monograph.

Are settlement patterns a meaningful problem of anthropological archaeology? Dale Henning has written (page 163) in his criticism of the Grant excavation that "The location of house outlines no longer constitutes a problem of good anthropological archaeology and has not for several decades." For a rebuttal I simply refer the reader to my published conclusions which are the first to correlate lineage residential units with Oneota summer occupations in longhouses which have not previously been described in the upper midwest. This is also the first Oneota monograph to attempt a demographic reconstruction of populations, and the first detailed survey of historic and ethnographic reports integrated with this one form of Oneota settlement pattern. I have made every reasonable effort to discuss alternatives and point out problems in Oneota archaeological correlations. There is a great deal more anthropology in this archaeological monograph than almost any other example from the midwest that Henning could have chosen; certainly more anthropological in approach than any study published by Henning; and apparently more anthropological in content than he proved capable of absorbing. I honestly do not know what he has in mind by saying that house outlines have not been a good anthropological problem for several decades. Several means more than two, so what he appears to be saying is we found out all we need to know about Oneota house outlines in the 1940s. As anyone acquainted with the history of research recognizes, this simply is not true, and as late as 1960 Griffin was postulating Oneota house form because of the lack of evidence. I do not know why Henning makes such slipshod, hasty, and ill-advised comments but they do not have the ring of scholarship to them, nor do they appear to me to show much contact with current, ongoing, Oneota research.

Excavation technique criticisms by Henning have to be evaluated in terms of his own research interests which are not illuminating about structural evidence. None of his Oneota site reports contain post mold patterns and presumably, sometime during his numerous excavations in various Oneota sites, he must have come across a line of post molds leading across his pit floor into backdirt. What decision did he make? What interpretations did he deduce from this kind of evidence? Did he actually think that it was not important because of non-existent Oneota house excavations he mistakenly thought were made "several decades" ago? It is not a convincing argument for Henning to categorically state that it should have taken at least five summers' work to clear the post lines, for he has never tried to do what he is suggesting, nor does it sound like he is interested in doing what he is suggesting. Frankly, I do not think it is possible to excavate and refill a small section each year and then re-excavate the lines the next, gradually expanding to eventually uncover a new and previously undescribed house type. Yearly re-excavation would require heavy equipment obliterating post evidence, or an increasing investment each year in hand-shoveled backdirt. The alternative, a huge open excavation for a five or more year period, is not acceptable to landowners, and sounds like it would be an irresponsible request. Because of the complexity of overlapping house lines a large area had to be cleared; and it was only then that enough lines could be established to isolate structures and search for the missing posts—some found, some not. In my opinion Henning is dead wrong when he condemns all use of site clearing by heavy equipment except in emergency salvage excavations. The point is not whether it is "good" or "bad," because value judgements on that level are meaningless. Rather, the question to be raised is whether the use of equipment and technique was appropriate to the problem being resolved. In this case the problem was raised by well-defined post lines cutting across the ten-foot wide B trench. Was it a house? Was it a fortification? Was it any definable feature? You now know the answer because the right decision was made to use techniques appropriate to finding out the answer. A balance had to be made between what potential information might be lost—both artifacts and structural evidence—against the value of finding out what the house type was like. We were enormously successful in finding answers to a number of significant questions. We did not answer all questions, and some remain half-resolved. But the early dates, a new pottery type, and the settlement pattern provides a basis for comparison which was greatly needed at the time the research was carried out.

Henning has raised a number of other points which I will answer briefly. Radiocarbon dates always raise problems, but the three dates for the Grant Village area are from Oneota, not Woodland features. The dates and cache pits are discussed on page 10, and table 1, page 76 shows the number of Oneota sherds found in each of the three storage pits. Pit 27 had one Woodland sherd in addition to 15 Oneota sherds, but this may well be a trade sherd since Woodland cultures were apparently continuing in adjacent regions (pages 2-4). This sherd was a cord-roughened, grit-tempered bodysherd without decoration. The three dates cluster well together, and fit consistently in terms of the twelve date sequence for the terrace (see figure 4). I see no reason to doubt the validity of the sequence at this time.

I would urge caution in accepting Henning's statement that all storage pits should be sluiced through 1/8 inch mesh. Where we are attempting to make paleontological correlations it is necessary to use windowscreen mesh to retain rodent teeth, rodents being climatically more diagnostic than other mammals. The Cahokia chronology presents great problems and I urge Henning to discuss it with Hall rather than relying on the 1966 MS by Hall. The artifact description in fact does not break with "standard" rubrics used as categories. The categories used in this report (see page 82) shaped stone, flaked stone, pottery, bone artifacts, shell artifacts, copper, and trade iron and glass, are not innovative or new, but as Henning will find out as he reads other archaeological reports, these terms are widely used . . . particularly pottery and flaked stone. The above terms are not newly minted, unexpected, or worth criticising in use. The celt-shaped stone tool is described; it was the only example found, and none has been found at other Allamakee County Oneota sites (page 46 and table 7, page 82). I urge Henning to review the celt-chisel problem. As he begins to look at collections of midwestern celts—as opposed to talking about them—he will notice that they usually show consistent battering at the butt end, much heavier use marks than the wear which appears on the sharpened edge. This suggests many of these celts were in fact chisels or wedges, being hammered, for example, by a billet of wood. All artifact categories are compared in terms of the general Oneota inventory from the Upper Iowa River (page 82) and the comparison is made to provide perspective. Thus, in answer to one of Henning's comments, I correctly stated pipes were rare, and correctly listed none occurred in the small Grant sample (pages 46,82). I correctly stated that the small tablet or charm had a grooved V-shaped decoration which "resembles the so-called 'turkey track'" (see page 47). I did not say it was a "turkey track" and I appropriately put "turkey track" in quotation marks giving the source of this petroglyph form from Orr. Not all of the "turkey tracks" follow the form stated by Henning, and there is an apparently related motif like that on the charm. The base of the only bison scapula in the Grant collection is illustrated in plate 27 and both the description (page 47) and the illustration mention and show the removal of the *spina scapulae*. I identified it as a scapula hoe—a common Oneota artifact type. Sickles are rare, none being identified in Orr's collections (page 82). If Henning wishes to rename this partial, broken scapula as a "bison scapula implement" rather than a "bison scapula hoe" because it conceivably might have been a "bison scapula sickle" I certainly have no disagreement about making this specific identification of a broken specimen more general. Nor do I really feel concern when, for the sake of argument, he reasons in just the opposite direction, that the "copper tubular ornament" in my report should be called a "copper tubular bead." The broken incomplete ornament (figure 29F) could certainly be called a bead as well as an ornament. This ornament was much more likely to have been a bead rather than a pendant, in the very same way that the scapula was much more likely to have been a hoe rather than a sickle.

The attitude of Dale Henning is far different from the other reviewers; and I think his remarks provide more insight into the state of his mind than they do into the state of the art.

The conclusions from my research are summarized on pages 62 to 65, and I will discuss these first, followed by a reply to points mentioned by individual contributors. Authors of comments are italicized; personal communications and references are in parentheses.

(1) *The Griffin hypothesis has been shown to be inapplicable in a major area of Oneota occurrence.* There is no challenge to the conclusion that Oneota longhouses appear early in the Upper Iowa Valley, and are different from the previously predicted wattle and daub house wall construction of Middle Mississippian derivation. *Glenn* has summarized new evidence that Middle Mississippian Muskogid crania differ from Oneota crania, providing another line of evidence for the separateness of the two traditions. *Peske* on the other hand provides additional examples of the Wisconsin Oneota, Carcajou Point houses. These have wall trench construction suggesting that this culture may be more closely similar in adaptation to Middle Mississippian than other Oneota cultures. Comments by *Baerreis, Brose, Davis, Hurley,* and *Peske* provide an interesting new range of information on Oneota house forms, from recently unpublished and published sources, except for the Quapaw problem which currently remains unresolved (see *Davis*), the houses reported generally follow the narrow oval pattern with pole frame construction. In general, Oneota and Middle Mississippian show few cultural interactions during the course of development of each tradition. The problem of Oneota cultural origins is becoming increasingly complicated, the problem being analogous to that of the origins of the Plains farmers (see *Bowers*). Because of differences in physical type *Glenn* sees no population origin from Muskogid Middle

Mississippian people. The formerly accepted cultural derivation of Oneota from Middle Mississippian has been increasingly challenged (Gibbon 1972), *Glenn,* and *Henning,* for various reasons, in part one suspects, because the Cahokia and Aztalan radiocarbon dates are later than anticipated. Robert Hall (personal communication) has recently raised questions over the Cahokia dates, but nevertheless there is no clear prototype for Oneota. *Peske* sees Oneota and Middle Mississippi development as related and concomitant, both heavily influenced by new lands for agriculture.

In summary, accumulating evidence shows that the Griffin hypothesis proved incorrect for at least one of three reasons (1) Oneota evolved separately and did not stem from what is currently defined as Middle Mississippian culture, or (2) the place of separation was so early and restricted in area that subsequent Oneota development, adaptation, and expansion has masked the original relationship, or because a crucial series of sites has not been excavated or (3) ceramic parallels have obscured the actual differences which always existed between the two traditions. Such explanations, and no doubt others which could be deduced, are mutually exclusive to varying degrees, and one might justifiably conclude that we now know the Griffin hypothesis is wrong, but we do not yet know for certain why it is wrong.

(2) The Longhouse type can be confirmed as present at the time of European explorations in many areas of the Mississippi. As reported by *Davis,* problems remain in correlating the huge Quapaw lodges seen by Joutel with archaeological sites and no conclusions can yet be drawn from the Arkansas data. In the Upper Mississippi Valley additional references can be mentioned which describe the large houses. For example, Medicine Bottle's Village is briefly described and illustrated as it appeared in 1850 by American artist, Henry Lewis (1957 edition: plate 13), on the Mississippi River in southern Minnesota. Eldon Johnson (personal communication) has told me of the reference by Major Long who describes another village of bark houses. I do not know how to interpret the Shea (1861) description of the early Le Sueur winter visit where four "cabins" were thrown into one for a banquet for 100 men. This is certainly an occasional pattern which could be prehistoric. The area weight of description favors the use of longhouses for seasonal summer settlements.

(3) *The longhouse abandonment can be documented among various tribes;* (4) *an explanation for the abandonment of this house type can be made;* and (5) *the origin of longhouses remains an unresolved question* were conclusions which no respondent discussed. Longhouse abandonment does not seem controversial, although the reasons leading to disuse of this form of housing may eventually be developed. I am certain no one would care to argue the reverse of point 5, for origin or origins cannot be clarified on the basis of present knowledge.

(6) *A summer residence pattern appears related to longhouse usage in the Mississippi Valley.* No reader challenged the basic ethnological and historical correlation, but some interesting problems were raised. The Le Sueur observation of a temporary winter banquet house *(Baerreis)* has been mentioned and *Peske* points up the important aspect of a residential village—it often served as a head-

quarters while family groups or hunters were away collecting food or obtaining other resources.

(7) *A village population was calculated.* The population estimate derived after assessing many imponderables and based upon a series of assumptions previously discussed, arrived at a village size of about 200 people. The ethnological analogy is based on the Iroquois parallel, not necessarily accurate but a reasonable choice. I was very interested that *Baerreis* recalculated the population on the Brose model, derived from a very different type of housing pattern, but which arrived at a somewhat higher population estimate. *Brose* asked about the derivation of House (?), which was projected from completing the circle of houses. Despite Henning's remarks about site destruction, about four-fifths of the acre site was left unexcavated and that whole sector was not tested in any way. In reply to another query by *Brose,* the north and east edge of the terrace obviously is important in projecting village size. I noted that the village boundary stopped before the terrace edge as seen in the B trench. Elsewhere the perimeter has to be projected, but I did not see any debris by the exposed edge elsewhere. I am of the opinion that the terrace edges have been quite stable. Excavation of the Hartley Fort edge boundary stockade showed it was still present, and much of the Lane Enclosure rampart on the eastern edge appears to be intact.

(8) *The Grant type is proposed as an Oneota archaeological manifestation.* There are extremely difficult problems in sampling which cannot be resolved at the present time. It is a type which will be expanded when other components are described. A preliminary survey of samples of Upper Iowa Oneota pottery from Ellison Orr's excavations, shows some of it has characteristics I would consider typical of the Grant type. I was interested in the comment by *Peske* that traits generally similar to those on Grant pottery have been documented on early Oneota pottery in Wisconsin. The problem of leached shell tempering mentioned by *Peske* should of course be re-evaluated during the subsequent identification of Grant components. Leaching was among the obvious and readily identified characteristics of the Grant pottery, and for this reason was included in the description.

(9) *The early dates and cultural succession on the terrace appear to answer a question raised about "pre-Oneota" Mississippian antecedents in this region.* There is clear Middle Mississippian influence in the late Woodland Hartley Fort, including trade sherds, triangular side-notched projectile points and possibly the idea of fortification. The cultural sequence as it is now known then shifts dramatically to a fully developed Oneota pattern with no observed Middle Mississippian influences. The question of Middle Mississippian and Oneota origins must be answered elsewhere.

In re-reading the comments there are a few final remarks which have not been included in the discussion of conclusions. The post mold diameter—as opposed to actual post size—mentioned by *Brose,* should certainly be re-evaluated.

Recent work (1971-1972) by John Hotopp at earthlodges of the Central Plains Tradition, Glenwood locality, has uncovered a great deal of structural evidence from excavations of 14 earthlodges along the highway right-of-way. He has commonly found charred post butts with no evidence of burning at a higher level on the lodge floor itself. He has interpreted this evidence as showing the trees for the posts were felled by repeatedly charring and chopping. The charred outer layer of the posts provides an index of the differential between post mold and actual post size, and he found differentials generally equivalent to those reported by *Brose*. The comment by *Baerreis* points up the need to study post molds to determine whether arched or straight-sided house walls are present. This evidence was missed because the ethnographic review followed rather than preceded the excavation and at the time I did not perceive that one of two distinct types might be present. The definition of longhouse has been questioned by *Peske*, and my position is that Iroquois longhouse excavations show rounded rather than square ends on the plans published by Ritchie (1965). Eldon Johnson (personal communication) has told me about his excavation of a protohistoric Oneota longhouse at Mille Lacs, but no other comparable finds have been brought to my attention, except for the note and photograph from *Field* who now believes he and Ellison Orr encountered one on the Flatiron Terrace but failed to recognize the post molds. His photograph of this salvage excavation seems to clearly show a row of substantial center post molds against the side wall of the excavation. The review of plains farmers by *Bowers* indicates that no survivals of the prairie bark lodges were known from that area. Finally, *Lounsbury* has further clarified the origin of the archaeological term Oneota.

ADDITIONAL REFERENCES

Bowers, Alfred W.
1950   *Mandan Social and Ceremonial Organization.* University of Chicago Press.

Brose, David S.
1970   The Summer Island Site: A Study of Prehistoric Cultural Ecology and Social Organization in the Northern Lake Michigan Area. *Case Western Reserve University, Studies in Anthropology,* no. 1.

Deitz, James
1965   The Dynamics of Cultural Change in Arikara Ceramics. *University of Illinois, Series in Anthropology,* no. 4, Urbana.

Gibbon, Guy E.
1969 MS The Walker-Hooper and Bornick Sites: Two Grand River Phase Oneota Sites in Central Wisconsin. Ph.D. Dissertation, University of Wisconsin, Madison.

1972   Cultural Dynamics and the Development of the Oneota Life-Way in Wisconsin. *American Antiquity,* vol. 37, no. 2:166-185, Menasha.

Glenn, Elizabeth J.
1971 MS The Physical Affiliations of the Oneota Peoples. Ph.D. Thesis, Department of Anthropology, Indiana University, Bloomington.

Harris, Sellig, and Voegelin, C. F.
1939   *Hidatsa Texts collected by Robert H. Lowie With Grammatical Notes and Phonographic Transcriptions,* Prehistoric Research Series, vol. 1, no. 6 Indiana Historical Society, Indianapolis.

Harvey, Amy Evelyn
1971 MS Challenge and Response: Environment and Northwest Iowa Oneota. Ph.D. Dissertation, University of Wisconsin, Madison.

Hurt, J. Wesley R.
1953   *Report of the Investigation of the Thomas Riggs Site 39HU1.* Archaeological Studies, Circular no. 5. South Dakota Archaeological Commission: Pierre.

Meleen, Elmer E.
      1949   Preliminary Report on the Thomas Riggs Village Site. *American Antiquity,* Vol. 14, no. 4, pt. 1, Menasha.

Shea, John Gilmary
      1861   *Early Voyages Up and Down the Mississippi by Cavelier, St. Cosme, Le Sueur, Gravier, and Guignas.* With an Introduction, Notes, and an Index. Albany.

Sperry, James E.
      1968   The Shermer Site 32EM10. *Plains Anthropologist: Journal of the Plains Conference* vol. 13, no. 42, pt. 2 Lawrence, Kansas.

Strong, William Duncan
      1940   *From History to Prehistory in the Northern Plains: Essays in Historical Anthropology of North America.* Smithsonian Miscellaneous Collections, vol. 100, Washington, D.C.

Thwaits, Reuben Gold (editor)
      1901   *The Jesuit Relations and Allied Documents,* vols. 10, 11, Cleveland. (Vols. issued 1897, 1898).

Will, George F. and Spinden, H. J.
      1906   *The Mandans: A Study of their Culture, Archaeology, and Ethnology.* Papers of the Peabody Museum of American Archaeology and Ethnology, vol. 3, no. 4, Cambridge: Harvard University, 1906.

Wood, W. Raymond
      1967   *An Interpretation of Mandan Culture History.* River Basin Survey Papers, bul. 198, Bureau of American Ethnology, Smithsonian Institution. Washington, D.C.

55 Flatiron Terrace Oneota Site, Upper Iowa River, Iowa, showing cut sections of pits and post molds, from H.P. Field photograph *circa* 1939-1941 (upper). Santee bark summer lodges. Medicine Bottle's Village, 1850, from Lewis 1957 edition, Segment of plate 13 (lower).

56   Discriminant Functions, Oneota and Varietal Series (from Glenn 1971 MS).

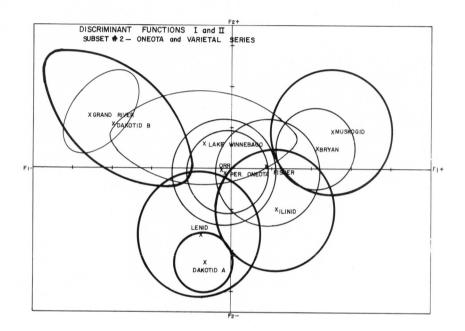

57   Discriminant Functions, Oneota Males and Females (from Glenn 1971 MS).

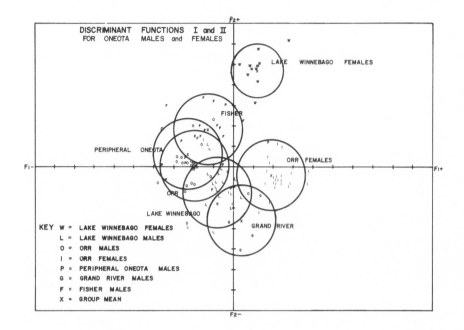